Legislative Apportionment

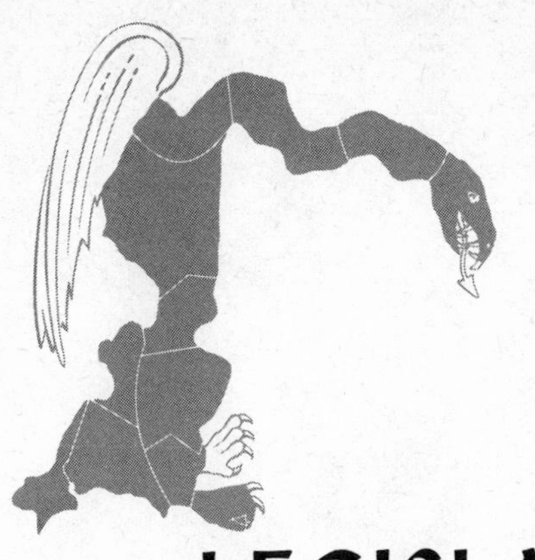

LEGISLATIVE APPORTIONMENT

Key to Power

EDITED BY HOWARD D. HAMILTON

HARPER & ROW, PUBLISHERS

NEW YORK, EVANSTON, AND LONDON

 For information address Harper & Row, Publishers, Incorporated, 49 East 33rd Street, New York 16, N.Y. 10016

LIBRARY OF CONGRESS CATALOG CARD NUMBER: 64-7649

C-1

PREFACE

THE REAPPORTIONMENT STRUGGLE, which had been waged furiously for a decade, and which by 1960 approached crisis proportions, came to a head on March 26, 1962, in the case of *Baker* v. *Carr*. The Supreme Court, which for sixteen years had consistently refused to intervene in a controversy so imbedded, as Justice Frankfurter said, in "the politics of the people," finally gave way to the pressure. It ruled that henceforth state legislative apportionments might be challenged under the "equal protection of the laws" guarantee of the Fourteenth Amendment. Two years later the Court took another giant step by applying Article I to open up to litigation Congressional districting patterns (*Wesberry* v. *Sanders,* February 17, 1964).

Baker v. *Carr,* the Tennessee reapportionment case referred to above, is undoubtedly one of the most important ever handed down by the Justices. It has brought on nationwide controversy, led to lawsuits by the score, and stimulated more apportionment activity —special sessions, new laws, constitutional amendments, and referenda—in two short years than in all the preceding decades of this century. It shattered ossified state apportionments, and, more importantly, it reopened serious thought on a subject which had called forth very little real questioning for generations. Now the whole topic is forced upon us, and Americans are obliged to rethink the theory and practice of representation on a scale unprecedented since the birth of the republic.

This little volume is designed to assist citizens, particularly collegians, to obtain the knowledge requisite to their own thinking about representation. The editor regards representation as a question perhaps preeminent among those timeless issues involved in the attempt to govern men democratically. This was certainly the view of the founding fathers, such as Thomas Jefferson, who protested the underrepresentation of the West in Virginia (interestingly, the more rural region), and inserted the guarantee of equal representation in the Northwest Ordinance. The importance of representation is obvious: government exercises power, almost plenary in the modern state, and apportionment is the way democracies distribute the keys to that power.

Baker v. *Carr* was the beginning of a long search for a settlement of basic issues; it decided jurisdictional rather than substantive questions. Hence this book allocates much space to the cases handed down more recently, which deal with apportionment standards and other substantive matters. Thus the reader is furnished the latest authoritative information, in the form of judicial opinions. According to official theory, the Court's decision regarding the constitutionality of any apportionment is not a judgment of its *wisdom* as a system of representation, but only a judgment as to whether an apportionment is compatible with the Constitution. As Justices Holmes and Frankfurter repeatedly insisted, constitutionality is not a synonym for wise public policy. Despite this official theory, Holmes is also authority for the contention that judges are not political eunuchs, either, and that their legal decisions inevitably partake of their political convictions.

I acknowledge the able assistance of my colleague, Dr. Robert D. Seltzer, and of my student, Mr. David Everson. I am especially indebted to Mr. Charles S. Rhyne, general counsel of the National Association of Municipal Law Officers, who wrote an original article, and to Rollin B. Posey, who conceived the idea of this book and expertly supervised every detail of its genesis.

Howard D. Hamilton

September, 1964

CONTENTS

PART IV

Where Do We Go From Here, How to Reapportion

PART V

Apportionment Standards

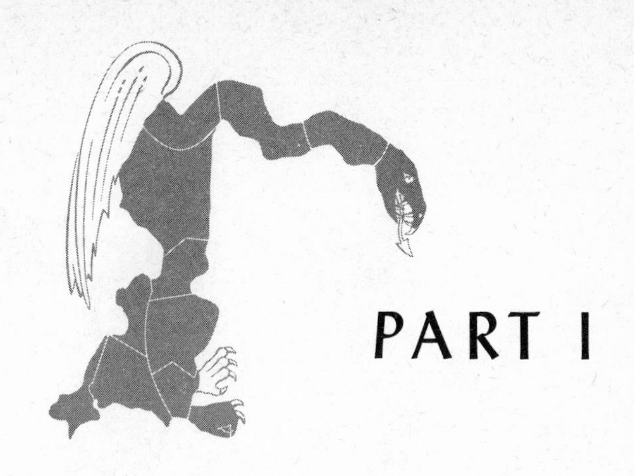

PART I

Origins of the Controversy

☆ 1 ☆

A NATIONAL COMMISSION LOOKS AT THE STATE LEGISLATURES

The Kestnbaum Commission

In a majority of states, city dwellers outnumber the citizens of rural areas. Yet in most states the rural voters are overwhelmingly in control of one legislative house, and overweighted if not dominant in the other. . . .

Reapportionment should not be thought of solely in terms of a conflict of interests between urban and rural areas. In the long run, the interests of all in an equitable system of representation that will strengthen state government is far more important than any temporary advantage to an area enjoying overrepresentation. . . .

One result of state neglect of the reapportionment problem is that urban governments have bypassed the states and made direct cooperative arrangements with the National Government in such fields as housing and urban development, airports, and defense community facilities. . . .

For these and other reasons, the Commission has come to the conclusion that the more the role of the states in our system is emphasized, the more important it is that the state legislatures be reasonably representative of all the people.

From *A Report to the President by the Commission on Intergovernmental Relations,* Meyer Kestnbaum, Chairman, June 1955, pp. 38-40.

☆ 2 ☆

UNREPRESENTATIVE STATES

Manning J. Dauer and Robert G. Kelsay

Some of the conditions that, by the 1950s, made reapportionment one of the most intense political issues in nearly every state, and gave rise to litigation culminating in Baker v. Carr are surveyed and measured in this influential article. Professors Dauer and Kelsay devised a technique for measuring the representativeness of legislatures which has been used extensively in subsequent literature and litigation. For example, a federal court ruled a 1963 Oklahoma law invalid, saying that an apportionment "where 31 percent of the people of the state would elect a majority of the house, brought about by adherence to arbitrary ceilings . . . is a denial of equal protection of the laws."

Tables 1 and 2 herein are not the original Dauer-Kelsay figures, but the comparable data as of July 1, 1961, as compiled by the National Municipal League. Thus these were the current data when the Supreme Court decided the Baker case. The 1961 tables differ only slightly from the 1955 figures. As one would expect, recalculation on the basis of the 1960 census showed most legislatures less representative than in 1955. Only a few states changed positions between 1955 and 1961, Oregon moving to the top of both tables and Alaska and Hawaii entering at the top of Table 2. By 1961, the already great disparities between the districts of most states had widened. Observe the number of chambers with disparities of

From *National Municipal Review,* December, 1955, pp. 571–575.

10 to 1, 50 to 1, 100 to 1, the senates of Alabama and California and the house in Connecticut and Vermont.

The problem of apportionment of our state legislatures is receiving increasing attention as the growth of American urban population continues. The importance of the issue is emphasized by the report of the Commission on Intergovernmental Relations. As matters now stand, the report points out, "Paradoxically enough, the interests of the urban areas are often more effectively represented in the national legislature than in their own state legislatures."

A number of studies of apportionment in individual states, of the methods of apportionment employed, and of the general problem of rural-urban representation have been made. Until now, however, no study has included an up-to-date index of representation showing the extent of the apportionment problem in all 48 states. That is the subject of the study discussed here, the results of which are shown in the accompanying tables.

The basic assumption of the study is that a legislature which does not equably represent the people of the state contains an innate weakness which limits the effective functioning of that government on many types of problems. It is assumed further that a measure of the representative character of the legislatures can be achieved by determining the smallest percentage of a state's population which could theoretically elect a majority of the lower house and a corresponding figure for the upper house under present district boundaries.

The resulting percentages allow the arrangement of the states in rank order from most representative to least representative. The figures for the upper house of each state are presented in Table 1 and those for the lower house in Table 2. A study of these tables reveals a definite correlation between the percentage figure and the difference between the district having the smallest ratio of population per representative and that with the largest ratio of population per representative.

A comparison of the figures in Tables 1 and 2 with those in the

TABLE 1

APPORTIONMENT OF STATE SENATES, JULY 1, 1961

Rank Order	State	Minimum Percentage of Population Needed to Elect Majority	Average Population per Senator	Largest Population per Senator	Smallest Population per Senator
1	Oregon	47.8	58,956	69,634	29,917
2	Missouri	47.7	127,058	155,683	96,477
3	Vermont	47.0	12,996	18,606	2,927
4	Maine	46.9	28,508	45,687	16,146
5	West Virginia	46.7	58,138	252,925	74,384
6	New Hampshire	45.3	25,288	41,457	15,829
7	Wisconsin	45.0	119,780	208,343	74,293
8	Massachusetts	44.6	128,714	199,107	86,355
9	Arkansas	43.8	51,036	80,993	35,983
10	Kentucky	42.0	79,951	131,906	45,122
11	Ohio	41.0	288,073	493,000	228,000
12	Indiana	40.4	93,250	171,089	39,011
13	Minnesota	40.1	50,953	99,446	26,458
14	South Dakota	38.3	19,443	43,287	10,039
15	Virginia	37.7	99,174	285,194	51,637
16	New York	36.9	287,626	425,276	190,343
17	North Carolina	36.9	91,123	272,111	45,031
18	Nebraska	36.6	32,822	51,757	18,824
19	Iowa	35.2	55,110	266,314	29,696
20	Alaska	35.0	11,308	57,431	4,603
21	Mississippi	34.6	44,452	126,502	14,314
22	Washington	33.9	58,229	145,180	20,023
23	Connecticut	33.4	70,423	175,940	26,297
24	Pennsylvania	33.1	226,387	553,154	51,793
25	Louisiana	33.0	83,513	248,427	31,175
26	North Dakota	31.9	12,907	42,041	4,698
27	Texas	30.3	309,022	1,243,158	147,454
28	Colorado	29.8	50,113	127,520	17,481
29	Michigan	29.0	200,682	690,259	55,806
30	Illinois	28.7	173,812	565,300	53,500
31	Tennessee	26.9	108,093	237,905	39,727
32	Wyoming	26.9	12,225	30,074	3,062
33	Kansas	26.8	54,465	343,231	16,083
34	Alabama	25.1	93,278	634,864	15,417
35	Oklahoma	24.5	52,916	346,038	13,125
36	South Carolina	23.6	51,796	216,382	8,629
37	Hawaii[a]	23.4	8,082	14,796	3,397
38	Georgia	22.6	73,021	556,326	13,050
39	Delaware	22.0	26,193	70,000	4,177
40	Utah	21.3	35,625	64,760	9,408
41	New Jersey	19.0	288,894	923,545	48,555
42	Rhode Island	18.1	18,684	47,080	486
43	Idaho	16.6	15,163	93,460	915
44	Montana	16.1	12,049	79,016	894
45	Maryland	14.2	106,920	492,428	15,481
46	New Mexico	14.0	29,719	262,199	1,874
47	Arizona	12.8	46,506	331,755	3,868
48	Florida	12.0	130,304	935,047	9,543
49	California	10.7	392,930	6,038,771	14,294
50	Nevada	8.0	16,781	127,016	568

[a] Based on registered voters.

SOURCE: National Municipal League, *Compendium on Legislative Apportionment* (1962 ed.).

TABLE 2

APPORTIONMENT OF LOWER HOUSES, JULY 1, 1961

Rank Order	State	Minimum Percentage of Population Needed to Elect Majority	Average Population per Representative	Largest Population per Representative	Smallest Population per Represent-ative
1	Alaska	49.0	5,654	6,605	2,945
2	Oregon	48.1	29,478	39,660	18,995
3	Hawaii[a]	47.8	3,962	4,679	2,257
4	New Jersey	46.5	101,113	143,913	48,555
5	Rhode Island	46.5	8,594	18,977	486
6	South Carolina	46.2	19,214	29,490	8,629
7	Massachusetts	45.3	21,452	49,478	3,559
8	California	44.7	196,465	306,191	72,105
9	Michigan	44.0	71,120	135,268	34,006
10	New Hampshire	43.9	1,517	1,179	8
11	North Dakota	40.2	5,499	8,408	2,655
12	Wisconsin	40.0	39,528	87,486	19,651
13	West Virginia	40.0	18,604	252,925	4,391
14	Illinois	39.9	56,956	160,200	34,433
15	Maine	39.7	6,418	13,102	2,394
16	Texas	38.6	62,864	105,725	33,987
17	South Dakota	38.5	9,074	16,688	3,531
18	New York	38.2	111,882	190,343	14,974
19	Pennsylvania	37.7	53,902	139,293	4,485
20	Virginia	36.8	39,669	142,597	20,071
21	Montana	36.6	7,178	12,537	894
22	Wyoming	35.8	5,894	10,024	2,930
23	Washington	35.3	28,820	57,648	12,399
24	Nevada	35.0	7,710	12,525	568
25	Indiana	34.8	46,623	79,538	14,804
26	Minnesota	34.5	26,060	99,446	8,343
27	Kentucky	34.1	30,382	67,789	11,364
28	Louisiana	34.1	31,019	120,205	6,909
29	Arkansas	33.3	17,863	31,686	4,927
30	Utah	33.3	13,916	32,380	1,164
31	Idaho	32.7	10,590	15,576	915
32	Colorado	32.1	26,984	63,760	7,867
33	Ohio	30.3	70,850	97,064	10,274
34	Oklahoma	29.5	19,242	62,787	4,496
35	Mississippi	29.1	15,558	59,542	3,576
36	Tennessee	28.7	36,031	79,031	3,454
37	North Carolina	27.1	37,968	82,059	4,520
38	New Mexico	27.0	14,394	29,133	1,874
39	Iowa	26.9	25,532	133,157	7,910
40	Alabama	25.7	30,818	104,767	6,731
41	Maryland	25.3	29,290	82,071	6,541
42	Georgia	22.2	19,235	185,422	1,876
43	Missouri	20.3	26,502	52,970	3,960
44	Kansas	18.5	17,428	68,646	2,069
45	Delaware	18.5	12,751	58,228	1,643
46	Connecticut	12.0	8,623	81,089	191
47	Florida	12.0	52,122	311,682	2,868
48	Vermont	11.6	1,585	33,155	38
49	Arizona	na	16,277	30,438	5,754

[a] Based on registered voters. Nebraska has unicameral legislature.
na: not available.
SOURCE: National Municipal League, *Compendium on Legislative Apportionment* (1962 ed.).

tabulation for 1937 shows that the situation is growing worse in most of the states. Some have improved markedly, Missouri and Illinois for example, but most of the states have failed to adjust to the increase in population and the urbanization of population. The state-by-state comparison shows that only ten of the 48 states have improved the representative nature of their upper houses. The remaining 38 have declined in representativeness. Similar figures for the 46 states on which data are available for lower houses show that only eleven have higher minimum percentages electing a majority than in 1937, while 35 have lower percentages for 1955 in comparison with 1937. In many cases the decline in percentage electing the house is after reapportionment measures have been adopted by the states in question following both the 1940 and 1950 censuses.

Some flagrant examples of changes in this period are found in Table 3.

Ranking of States

To get a single index of the representative nature of the entire legislative body, i.e., the representativeness of the two houses combined, one may compare the relative rankings of each house for a state in Tables 1 and 2. If this is done, in descending order from the top, Massachusetts, Virginia, Oregon, Wisconsin, and West Virginia rank highest. At the bottom, and again in descending order are Connecticut, Maryland, Delaware, Nevada, and Florida.

There are recognized limitations to this method of ranking the states, however. One house that is considered to be truly representative does not necessarily offset a most unrepresentative second house. A state with reasonably adequate representation in both houses might rank approximately the same. But legislation affecting urban areas, for example, might have a relatively easier chance of passage in the latter case than in the former, which raises some doubt as to the validity of such rankings. Nevertheless, this combined ranking probably does have some validity at least for the states at the top and bottom of the scale.

TABLE 3

EXAMPLES OF CHANGES IN PERCENTAGES OF POPULATION ELECTING MAJORITIES IN STATE LEGISLATURES, 1937 AND 1955

State	Chamber	1937 Percentage Electing Majority	1955 Percentage Electing Majority
New Hampshire	Senate	50.6	44.7
	House	50.2	37.4
Delaware	Senate	21.7	22.7
	House	32.9	19.4
Connecticut	Senate	44.9	36.5
	House	8.7	9.6
New York	Senate	43.9	40.9
	House	51.9	37.1
Nevada	Senate	26.6	12.4
	House	18.6	28.8
California	Senate	12.5	11.9
	House	47.6	44.7
Florida	Senate	26.1	17.7
	House	23.5	17.2
Maryland	Senate	18.1	15.5
	House	33.6	27.6

Certain generalized observations can be made as to why a state is high or low in the listings. The worst situations exist in those states where a constitutional or statutory limitation sets a rigid system which recognizes some unit of local government as the basis of representation, such as the town or county. Connecticut, for example, elects at least one representative from each town, while in Nevada one senator is elected from each county.

Along with using a local unit as an area of representation, some states ranking low establish rigid representation ratios. In these instances no one unit can have more than a certain number of legislators, thereby disregarding the relative difference in size between the largest and smallest units. Thus the Florida constitution establishes a ratio of three to one between the largest and smallest counties for representation, although the counties range in population from nearly 500,000 down to 2,000. Several variations of such rigid limitations could be mentioned, but invariably they have the effect of giving sparsely populated areas considerable overrepresentation.

☆ *3* ☆

POWER OF RURAL VOTE

Ralph Eisenberg

Was the picture depicted by Dauer and Kelsay changed significantly by reapportionments following the 1960 census? This article answers that question and also measures the "devaluation of the urban vote" from 1910 to 1960. What factors account for the failure of the post-1960 apportionments to alter that trend? Most state constitutions specify reapportionment, usually for both chambers, after each census, but it often does not occur. Note that Dr. Eisenberg uses a different statistical method for measuring the representativeness of legislatures.

With the consequences of the U.S. Supreme Court's decision in Tennessee's *Baker* v. *Carr* case being felt in many states, it is appropriate to bring up to date statistics on national averages of the relative values of the right to vote for state legislative representation. Such data were published in late 1961 and proved useful to demonstrate the extent of malapportionment. The revised statistics demonstrate the impact of reapportionment upon the underrepresentation of urban and suburban voters that the 1960 census exposed.

Enough reapportionments occurred from the time of the 1960 census to the announcement of the *Baker* decision to permit the modification of the national averages previously calculated on the basis of 1960 census figures but before any reapportionments or redistrictings based upon the census results. There were 25 states

From *National Municipal Review,* October, 1962, pp. 489–492, 530.

by March 26, 1962, in which some reapportionment or redistricting was effected for the decade of the '60s. The changes that occurred were the result of automatic changes in representation dictated by constitutional provisions, or legislative enactments that reapportioned representation in either one or both houses of a legislature, or the product of nonlegislative agencies as provided by state constitutions or statutes.

The research in which Paul T. David and I were involved for over a year produced statistics that indicated a historic trend since 1910 in the devaluation of the value of the vote possessed by citizens of urban and, more lately, suburban counties. These studies measured the adequacy of legislative representation by employing a tool that demonstrated the extent to which representation deviated from norms of ideal population size per representative in each legislative house in each state. The effect of these deviations upon urban and rural voters was measured by grouping all counties in the country into four categories of population size. The national average of the relative values of the right to vote in the most rural counties increased from 113 percent in 1910 to 171 percent in 1960, while the national averages in the most urban counties decreased from 81 percent in 1910 to 76 percent in 1960.

Since publication of those figures, we applied the previous data collected for representation and the 1960 census to the changes in representation brought about by state legislative reapportionments enacted prior to the *Baker* decision. We sought to investigate two additional aspects of apportionment. First, we wished to determine if the historic trends in increasing overrepresentation of rural counties and increasing underrepresentation of urban counties detected from 1910 through 1950, after reapportionments for those decades, continued to be evident following the initial reapportionments after the 1960 census. Secondly, we sought to determine how much the inequities of legislative representation in the states, and nationally, revealed by newly published census data were reduced by reapportionments.

The results are not surprising. First, the trends toward increasing overrepresentation of rural counties and increasing underrepresentation of the urban counties as displayed in the national averages continued through March, 1962. The data in the accompanying table demonstrate this phenomenon in the contrast between the relative values of the vote in the four categories of counties for 1950 and after reapportionments for 1960.

RELATIVE VALUES OF THE RIGHT TO VOTE FOR REPRESENTATIVES IN STATE LEGISLATURES—NATIONAL AVERAGES

Categories of Counties by Population Size	1950 Census	1960 Census Before Reapportionments	1960 Census After Reapportionments
Under 25,000	141%	171%	168%
25,000 to 99,999	114	123	121
100,000 to 49,999	83	81	83
500,000 and over	78	76	77

Secondly, the 25 reapportionments or redistrictings failed to modify the inequities of overrepresentation and underrepresentation that the census revealed. By comparing the 1960 figures for the pre- and post-reapportionment averages, it is obvious that the general effect of the reapportionment was small. The extremes of under- and overrepresentation that existed prior to reapportionments were only slightly reduced.

Thus, the reapportionment efforts of state legislatures, where they occurred, did not contribute to any significant improvement in the relative vote values of urban and suburban citizens. The continual worsening of their relative political power since 1910 was not arrested and the particular inequities created by population movements during the past decade were not remedied.

The reasons for the limited effect of reapportionments upon underrepresentation of urban and suburban counties are not hard to find or illustrate. Of the 25 reapportionments, only seven affected both legislative chambers; and in only one of the seven did the redistricting decrease the long-term disparities in representation between urban and rural counties by comparison with 1950. In the other six states the reapportionments left the most urban counties more underrepresented than after 1950 and the most rural counties more overrepresented. Eighteen states reapportioned only one legislative chamber; all but four of these were lower houses. Fourteen of them resulted in a continued exaggeration of the over- and underrepresentation under way since 1910. . . .

The continuing trend of urban underrepresentation in states that were reapportioned took place despite adherence by most of them to constitutional standards for legislative representation. Constitutional biases often are responsible for the situation of inequitable representation in both legislative houses or in at least one house. For example, states whose representation system is the "federal" form are obligated to reapportion only one house of the legislature and that house only within guarantees of minimum representation per county. Such provisions leave rural areas solidly entrenched in control of one house and overrepresented in the other, even where urban areas control majorities in the second house. . . .

. . .

Other states that employ population as an ostensible apportionment standard do so within limits that reward the least populated counties proportionately more than the most populated counties. Georgia is a notable example of this type of situation. In the lower house each of the 159 counties has one representative but additional representation is given to the 38 most populous counties; yet three is the maximum number that any county may have. . . .

Another group of states either ignores relatively clear constitutional instructions to distribute representation by population or takes advantage of general constitutional language by enacting only token reapportionments. Virginia's recent redistricting acts typify this category of action. Louisiana also used a token approach as it amended its constitution merely to add four seats to its upper house and allot them to two badly underrepresented suburban counties. But the four seats still were less than those counties merited. . . .

. . .

A final example illustrates how effective reapportionment was and can be brought about. By any standard of adequate representation with population as a primary apportionment criterion, Oregon put into effect the best reapportionment based upon the 1960 census. This was possible because of a recent constitutional amendment that made the state supreme court the final arbiter of legislative reapportionment. In exact accordance with the steps anticipated by that amendment, the legislature enacted a redistricting measure; the supreme court found it deficient and ordered the Secretary of State to devise a new redistricting plan to be submitted to the court for approval; the Secretary of State submitted a plan that the court returned for two alterations before giving its approval to the measure. The Oregon court was guided by the constitutional prescription of population as the apportionment standard for both houses.

It is clear that where reapportionments were enacted following the 1960 census, without the stimulus of the *Baker* decision, they produced only minimal shifts in representation that did not remedy urban underrepresentation. Reluctance on the part of legislators to execute their reapportionment obligations is not solely responsible for this result. Constitutional standards for apportionment that favor rural counties are even more basic causes of malapportionment. Now that courts are entertaining allegations of inequitable representation, many of the biases contained in constitutional standards for apportionment ultimately may be invalidated as they must be if more equitable representation is to be realized.

PART II

The Reapportionment Battle in the Courts

☆ 4 ☆

LITIGATION IN STATE COURTS:

Fergus v. Marks

The disparities in representation, documented and measured in the preceding articles, inevitably have motivated residents of underrepresented districts to seek relief in the courts. Prior to World War II, the litigation was in state courts, seeking to compel legislatures to comply with the apportionment obligations and standards of their respective state constitutions. Observe the Illinois standards outlined below, which are typical of the provisions of state constitutions to assure regular and equitable apportionment. Some constitutions, like that of Indiana, require reapportionment every five or six years. In the nineteenth century suits usually attacked gerrymandering; in the twentieth century they have been concerned with legislative defaults (e.g., Illinois from 1901 to 1957, Indiana from 1921 to 1963) and systematic underrepresentation of urban or metropolitan areas.

Most state courts did not take the (apparent) position of the federal courts prior to 1962, that districting is a "political question," which is to say nonjusticiable, and frequently gerrymanders were held invalid—five times in Indiana. Nevertheless, litigation in state courts usually has been futile because of one of the following obstacles: (1) State courts usually will not invalidate an apportionment law unless a previous one can be revived simultaneously, feeling that the state must not be left without any districting system—that the cure would be worse than the disease. (Cf. Justice Frank-

321 Ill. 510 (1926).

furter in Colegrove.) (2) Even if an inequitable law can be overturned, reversion to an earlier one would make the situation worse, the dilemma in Indiana and many states. (3) State courts will not issue a writ of mandamus to a defaulting legislature, as in the instant case.

Every conceivable legal angle was explored in Illinois—in vain. The courts refused to restrain payment of legislators' salaries, to grant writs of quo warranto or mandamus, or to question the validity of the laws enacted by a legislature sitting under an obsolete apportionment. The Fergus case is the leading state case, cited as authority by courts all over the nation. Queries: Did the decision rest on "legal principles" or something else? Was it derived from sound logic or circular reasoning?

Petition by John B. Fergus for a writ of mandamus to compel Adolph Marks and others, as members of the General Assembly, to meet and apportion the state into senatorial districts.

HEARD, J. Section 6 of Article IV of the Illinois constitution provides:

> The General Assembly shall apportion the state every ten years . . . by dividing the population of the state, as ascertained by the federal census, by the number of fifty-one, and the quotient shall be the ratio of representation in the senate. The state shall be divided into fifty-one senatorial districts, each of which shall elect one senator. . . . Senatorial districts shall be formed of contiguous and compact territory, bounded by county lines, and contain as nearly as practicable an equal number of inhabitants; but no district shall contain less than four-fifths of the senatorial ratio.

In accordance with this provision, the General Assembly in 1901 passed an apportionment act, since which time it has failed or neglected to comply with this constitutional provision and its members are still elected under the act of 1901. The petitioner, by leave of this court, has filed his petition herein asking this court to issue the people's writ of mandamus to compel the respondents to meet and apportion the state. . . .

Petitioner contends that the duty imposed by the people upon the General Assembly to apportion the state after each federal census is clear and unmistakable, and the provisions of the constitution are mandatory in this respect. The right which the petitioner sets up as the basis for the relief sought is the right of representation, which by the Declaration of Independence is said to be a right estimable to the people and formidable only to tyrants.

The writ of mandamus is a summary writ issuing from a court of competent jurisdiction, commanding the officer or body to whom it is addressed to perform some specific duty which the relator is entitled, of right, to have performed and which the party owing the duty has failed to perform. In *Marbury* v. *Madison,* 1 Cranch. 137 (a leading case on the subject of the right of mandamus against the executive branch), it is said: "Still to render the mandamus a proper remedy, the officer to whom it is directed must be one to whom, on legal principles, such writ may be directed."

From an inspection of the pleadings, it is apparent that the duty that is sought to be compelled is unmistakable, so the only question to be determined is whether or not, on legal principles, the writ of mandamus can be issued directed to respondents in their official capacity.

By Article III of the Illinois constitution, the powers of the government are divided into three distinct departments—legislative, executive, and judicial—and no person or collection of persons, being one of these departments, may exercise any power properly belonging to either of the others, except as expressly directed or permitted by the constitution. Neither of these three departments is subordinate to or may exercise any control over another except as is provided by the constitution. . . .

In *People* v. *Dunne,* 258 Ill. 441, a case involving the right of the judicial department to compel by mandamus a coordinate department to act, this court, speaking through that great jurist, Mr. Justice Cartwright, made a careful and exhaustive résumé of the authorities, and among other things said:

". . . where final action upon any subject was confided to either of the other departments, there the responsibility must rest of conforming such action to the law and the Constitution; that the court had no power to compel either of the other departments of the government to perform any duty which the Constitution might impose upon them, no matter how palpable such duty might be."

The court held that the decisions of this court were uniform, and that the judicial department had no jurisdiction to award writs of mandamus against a coordinate department of the state government and cited the following authorities: . . .

This court has observed with sedulous care the principles announced in the cases above cited, and has consistently declined to encroach upon the powers granted by the Constitution to the Legislature, and has never arrogated to itself the right to pass upon the wisdom or propriety of legislative acts within such powers. The duty to reapportion the state is a specific legislative duty imposed solely upon the legislative department, and it alone is responsible to the people for a failure to perform that duty.

It is contended by petitioner that, even though this court may not be able to compel the Legislature to redistrict the state in any particular manner, the duty upon respondents to apportion being clear, the court can mandamus them to act in the premises. It is ordinarily the rule that an officer clothed with discretion as to the manner in which he will perform his duty, who fails to perform that duty, may be compelled by mandamus to act, the court simply compelling action and not the manner of action. This rule, however, applies only to officers to whom, on legal principles, the writ of mandamus may be directed, and, as the judicial department cannot compel by mandamus the legislative department to perform any duty imposed upon it by law, it can have no application in this case.

This court, being debarred by the constitutional division of governmental functions from compelling by mandamus the performance of a duty by the legislative department, the relief prayed for cannot be granted, and the writ is denied.

☆5☆

LITIGATION IN FEDERAL COURTS:

Colegrove v. Green

After repeated failure to secure satisfaction from legislatures or state courts, citizens of Illinois and other states turned—after World War II—to the federal judiciary, arguing that the extreme disparities in representation under which they suffered contravened the Fourteenth Amendment's "equal protection" clause: "No State shall . . . deny to any person within its jurisdiction the equal protection of the laws." The patterns of malrepresentation, both for legislatures and for the United States House of Representatives, were largely attributable to failures of legislatures to redistrict for decades—even generations. Indeed, legislative inaction added a new term to our political vocabulary, "silent gerrymander." Even in cases where redistricting did take place, restrictive state constitutional provisions often prevented significant relief.

Although Professor Colegrove's suit attacked the Illinois congressional districting pattern (see facts in the dissenting opinion), Justice Frankfurter's arguments were also applicable to suits challenging state legislative districting, and during the sixteen years after Colegrove, the court routinely rejected such suits, using terse per curiam memoranda citing Colegrove. Thus it takes its place with Baker v. Carr as a landmark case. Another was added when, on February 17, 1964, the court in Wesberry v. Sanders ruled (in a Georgia case) that Article I, sections 2 and 4 of the Constitution allow federal courts to take jurisdiction of suits attacking inequit-

328 U.S. 549 (1946).

able congressional districting. With the Colegrove decision thus, in effect, reversed, Justice Black's 1946 dissenting opinion became, in 1964, that of the court.

The Colegrove decision was an anomalous one; the court was short two members (one abroad, one recently deceased), and Justice Rutledge, the fourth member of the majority, wrote an independent opinion. He agreed with the dissenters that the suit should not be classified as nonjusticiable, but voted to dismiss for other reasons. Thus there was a majority decision but no "opinion of the Court." The result was confusion and general misunderstanding of the case, shared equally by the public and the federal judiciary. It was this anomaly which enabled Justice Brennan in the Baker case to make the claim that the two decisions were consistent—a claim which provoked bitter dissents. Note the two distinctly different reasons which Justice Frankfurter advanced for denying relief. Which would have the wider significance? Did Frankfurter, who frequently reprimanded his colleagues for obiter dicta (superfluous comments), engage in it here? How efficacious are the nonjudicial remedies which he commends to the appellants? Did the two sets of judges arrive at their positions by legal ratiocination or by value judgments?

MR. JUSTICE FRANKFURTER announced the judgment of the Court and an opinion in which Mr. Justice Reed and Mr. Justice Burton concurred. . . .

We are of opinion that appellants ask of this Court what is beyond its competence to grant. This is one of those demands on judicial power which cannot be met by verbal fencing about "jurisdiction." It must be resolved by considerations on the basis of which this Court, from time to time, has refused to intervene in controversies. It has refused to do so because due regard for the effective working of our government revealed this issue to be of a peculiarly political nature and therefore not meet for judicial determination.

This is not an action to recover damage because of the discriminatory exclusion of a plaintiff from rights enjoyed by other citizens. The basis for this suit is not a private wrong, but a wrong suffered by Illinois as a polity. In effect this is an appeal to the federal courts to reconstruct the electoral process of Illinois in order that it may be adequately represented in the councils of the Nation. Because the Illinois legislature has failed to revise its districts in order to reflect great changes, during more than a generation, in the distribution of its population, we are asked to do this, as it were, for Illinois.

Of course no court can affirmatively remap the Illinois districts so as to bring them more in conformity with the standards of fairness for a representative system. At best we could only declare the existing system invalid. The result would be to leave Illinois undistricted and to bring into operation, if the Illinois legislature chose not to act, the choice of members for the House of Representatives on a state-wide ticket. The last stage may be worse than the first. The upshot of judicial action may defeat the political principle which led Congress, more than a hundred years ago to require districting. . . . Assuming acquiescence on the part of the authorities of Illinois in the selection of its Representatives by a mode that defies the direction of Congress, the House of Representatives may reject a delegation of Representatives-at-large. . . . Nothing is clearer than that this controversy concerns matters that bring courts into immediate and active relations with party contests. From the determination of such issues this Court has traditionally held aloof. It is hostile to a democratic system to involve the judiciary in the politics of the people. And it is no less pernicious if such judicial intervention in an essentially political contest is dressed up in the abstract phrases of the law.

The appellants urge with great zeal that the conditions of which they complain are grave evils and offend public morality. The Constitution gives ample power to provide against these evils. But due regard for the Constitution as a viable system precludes judicial correction. Authority for dealing with such problems resides elsewhere. Article I, section 4 of the Constitution provides that "The Times, Places and Manner of holding Elections for . . . Representatives, shall be prescribed in each State by the Legislature thereof; but the Congress may at any time by Law make or alter such

Regulations." The short of it is that the Constitution has conferred upon Congress exclusive authority to secure fair representation by the states in the popular House and left to that House determinations whether states have fulfilled their responsibility. . . .

To sustain this action would cut very deeply into the very being of Congress. Courts ought not enter this political thicket. The remedy for unfairness in districting is to secure legislatures that will apportion properly, or to invoke the ample powers of Congress. The Constitution has many commands that are not enforceable by courts because they clearly fall outside the conditions and purposes that circumscribe judicial action. . . . The Constitution has left the performance of many duties in our governmental scheme to depend on the fidelity of the executive and legislative action and, ultimately, on the vigilance of the people in exercising their political rights.

Dismissal of the complaint is affirmed.

Mr. Justice Black (Mr. Justice Douglas and Mr. Justice Murphy concurring with him) dissenting: . . .

It is difficult for me to see why the 1901 State Apportionment Act does not deny appellants equal protection of the laws. The failure of the legislature to reapportion the districts for forty years, despite census figures indicating great changes in the distribution of the population, has resulted in districts the populations of which range from 112,000 to 900,000. One of the appellants lives in a district of more than 900,000 people. His vote is consequently much less effective than that of each citizen living in the district of 112,000. And such a gross inequality in the voting power of citizens irrefutably demonstrates a complete lack of effort to make an equitable apportionment. The 1901 Act would thus result in a wholly indefensible discrimination against appellants and all other voters in heavily populated districts. The equal protection clause of the Fourteenth Amendment forbids such discrimination. No one would deny that the equal protection clause would prohibit a law that would expressly give certain citizens a half-vote and others a full-vote. . . .

While the Constitution contains no express provision requiring that congressional districts contain approximately equal populations, the constitutionally guaranteed right to vote and the right to have one's vote counted clearly imply the policy that state election systems, no matter what their form, should be designed to give approximately equal weight to each vote cast. To some extent this implication of Article I is expressly stated by section 2 of the Fourteenth Amendment which provides that "Representatives shall be apportioned among the several States according to their respective numbers. . . ." The purpose of this requirement is obvious: It is to make the votes of the citizens of the several states equally effective in the selection of members of Congress. It was intended to make illegal a nationwide "rotten borough" system as between the states. The policy behind it is broader than that. It prohibits as well congressional "rotten boroughs" within the states, such as the ones here involved.

. . . What is involved here is the right to vote guaranteed by the Federal Constitution. It has always been the rule that where a federally protected right has been invaded the federal courts will provide the remedy to rectify the wrong done. Federal courts have not hesitated to exercise their equity powers in cases involving deprivation of property and liberty. There is no reason why they should do so where the case involves the right to choose representatives that make laws affecting liberty and property. . . .

☆ 6 ☆

THE FEDERAL COURTS SHOULD ACT

Anthony Lewis

The Colegrove decision, particularly Justice Frankfurter's thesis that the courts should remain entirely aloof—not enter that "political thicket"—evoked extensive criticism in legal journals which surely contributed to the Supreme Court's subsequent about face. After criticizing Colegrove on a variety of grounds, Anthony Lewis concluded with the following statement of the practical reasons for judicial intervention.

The philosophy underlying the opinion in *Colegrove* v. *Green* is summed up in one sentence of the opinion: "It is hostile to a democratic system to involve the judiciary in the politics of the people." The argument is that in a democracy excessive reliance on the courts weakens the responsibility of the legislature and of the voters. And so those injured by unfair districts are remitted to the state legislatures and to Congress for relief. If this is not a cynical resolution of the problem—and surely it is not so intended—its premise must be that there is a reasonable chance of action in the legislative branches. But the historical evidence indicates that there is no basis whatsoever for this premise.

Legislative fairness in districting is inhibited by factors built into our political structure. Once a group has the dominant position—as the rural legislators generally have—its overriding interest is to maintain that position. The motives of most individual legislators are just as selfish. Any substantial change in districts means that the members must face new constituents and deal with uncertainties—in short undergo risks that few politicians would voluntarily put upon themselves. Voting for a fair apportionment bill would in many cases mean voting oneself out of office. That is too much to ask of most politicians. The result is that the state legislatures do not reapportion fairly or, more commonly, do not reapportion at all.

Unequal districts have been a part of the American political scene, as Mr. Justice Frankfurter observed in *Colegrove*, for generations. Why, then, should the federal courts undertake at this time to deal with the problem? The preliminary observation may be made that no legitimate interests or expectations have become settled as a result of past judicial inaction. But there are affirmative reasons for intervention now by the federal courts.

First, the provisions of a Constitution drawn with "purposeful vagueness" have always been interpreted and enforced by the Supreme Court in accordance with the changing needs of government and society. Interests which at one time received no judicial protection have been given that protection when their importance emerged. It was almost sixty years, for example, before the Supreme Court found any protection for free speech in the Fourteenth Amendment.

The effects of malapportionment are much graver today than they were a century ago. In a day when the federal government subsisted primarily on tariff revenues, unequal representation could be regarded as an insignificant evil; government itself had a less significant impact on society. But when the federal and state governments spend a third of the national income, when they are relied upon to regulate every aspect of a complex industrial civilization, the consequences of unequal representation are correspondingly severe. The rapid growth of our population and change in its character make even more urgent the need for regular, equitable adjustment of representation.

Second, in weighing the appropriateness of judicial intervention, courts consider not only the gravity of the evil assailed but the unlikelihood of its correction by other means. This is the teaching of the Supreme Court's tentative efforts to outline a modern philosophy of judicial review. These efforts at articulation began with the suggestion by Mr. Justice Stone, in his footnote to *Carolene Products,* that courts should be "more exacting" in their view of restrictions on political liberties. Just before he went on the court, Robert H. Jackson commented:

> [W]hen the channels of opinion and of peaceful persuasion are corrupted or clogged, these political correctives can no longer be relied on, and the democratic system is threatened at its most vital point. In that event the Court, by intervening, restores the processes of democratic government; it does not disrupt them.

Particular formulations have been the subject of dispute, but there would seem to be general agreement in the Supreme Court today that what Mr. Justice Frankfurter has called "the indispensable conditions of a free society" deserve special judicial protection. Perhaps the most useful conception suggested so far is that courts should be free to step in when the political process provides no inner check, as in the case of legislation affecting interests which have no voice in the legislature.

The Supreme Court has applied these principles especially in the area of free speech. If speech by a dissident minority is of sufficient importance to the political health of society to deserve special judicial protection, surely there is greater warrant for intervention by the courts when "the streams of legislation become poisoned at the source." Of what use is the right of a minority—or a majority, as is often the case in malapportioned districts—to apply persuasion if the machinery of government prevents political change?

Malapportionment is a disease incurable by legislative physic. No one would suggest that the federal courts can provide a quick, complete remedy. What they have to offer is chiefly their educational and moral influence. Judge Wyzanski has said that the Supreme Court

> has perhaps been primarily an educational force rather than an absolute restraint. And no estimate of the role of the Court can overlook the contribution which judicial opinions have made to political thinking.

Judging by the available evidence, it appears that the political branches would respond to moral leadership from the judiciary on the apportionment issue. The benefits that the courts can bring to the process will follow from their merely taking jurisdiction and requiring argument on the merits. Perhaps a spirit of commonsense self-limitation would weigh against the federal courts' granting relief in many cases. But for the first time those responsible for unequal representation would have to seek a justification better than the mere possession of power.

The federal courts cannot remake politics. But they can be a conscience, expressing ideas which take root in public and political opinion. Americans have traditionally looked to the courts for moral values, as they have tended to think politically in terms of moral judgments. Whatever the merits, these are our traditions. Only by putting them to use, with the help of the federal courts, can we begin to solve the problem of unequal representation.

☆ 7 ☆

THE TENNESSEE CASE: *Baker v. Carr*

This case produced all the hubbub. "In terms of involvement of the judiciary in the politics of the people, and in the great questions of democratic institutional arrangements, the decision is second only to Marbury v. Madison," commented Professor Robert Dixon. Certainly it has given rise to more serious discussion of the theory and practice of democratic government than this country has known since the days of the Founding Fathers. The case engendered much controversy and heat within the court as well, since all but two (Warren and Black) of the eight participants wrote opinions, filling 164 pages of the United States Reports. Something of a bridge from Colegrove to Baker was the Tuskegee municipal boundary case, Gomillion v. Lightfoot (1961), which overturned a statute that artfully recast the city boundaries to place nearly all the Negro residents outside the city limits. In that case, however, Justice Frankfurter, for the Court, deliberately based the decision on the Fifteenth (Negro suffrage) Amendment rather than the equal protection clause of the Fourteenth, thereby awarding relief without disturbing Colegrove.

Baker v. Carr posed five major, and some minor, questions: (1) Is the suit within the jurisdiction of federal courts? (2) Is the issue "justiciable," that is, is it a controversy which is of a type which can be properly settled by judicial action? (3) Do the facts establish a denial of equal protection? (4) What standards of apportionment

369 U.S. 186 (1962).

are dictated by the equal protection principle? (5) What remedies may courts grant?

The Court chose to decide only the first two issues, and then remanded the case to the trial court. Hence the case left standing more issues than it settled. Crucial to the decision were the Court's reading of the significance of Colegrove and the per curiam decisions following it, and its definition of the "political question" concept. Note Justice Brennan's handling of these questions. Also notice the rebuttal of Justice Frankfurter, whose opinion came shortly before his illness and retirement. What, one may wonder, was the real reason Justice Stewart wrote his opinion? And what notions, as of 1962, did the respective justices have about apportionment criteria? The immensity of the task of constructing such criteria, and the initial confusions of the Court, are demonstrated by the difficulties of Justices Clark and Harlan in trying to evaluate the representativeness of the Tennessee districting system. Such problems lead to a question whether the Court should have ventured into the "political thicket" or "quagmire," as Justice Frankfurter has variously called it.

MR. JUSTICE BRENNAN delivered the opinion of the Court.

This civil action was brought under 42 U.S.C. §§ 1983 and 1988 to redress the alleged deprivation of federal constitutional rights. The complaint, alleging that by means of a 1901 statute of Tennessee apportioning the members of the General Assembly among the State's 95 counties, "these plaintiffs and others similarly situated, are denied the equal protection of the laws accorded them by the Fourteenth Amendment to the Constitution of the United States by virtue of the debasement of their votes," was dismissed by a three-judge court convened under 28 U.S.C. § 2281 in the Middle District of Tennessee. The court held that it lacked jurisdiction of the subject matter and also that no claim was stated upon which relief could be granted. 179 F. Supp. 824. We noted probable jurisdiction of the appeal. 364 U.S. 898. We hold that the dismissal was error, and remand the cause to the District Court for trial and further proceedings consistent with this opinion. . . .

JURISDICTION OF THE SUBJECT MATTER

The District Court was uncertain whether our cases withholding federal judicial relief rested upon a lack of federal jurisdiction or upon the inappropriateness of the subject matter for judicial consideration—what we have designated "nonjusticiability." The distinction between the two grounds is significant. In the instance of nonjusticiability, consideration of the cause is not wholly and immediately foreclosed; rather, the Court's inquiry necessarily proceeds to the point of deciding whether the duty asserted can be judicially identified and its breach judicially determined, and whether protection for the right asserted can be judicially molded. In the instance of lack of jurisdiction the cause either does not "arise under" the Federal Constitution, laws or treaties (or fall within one of the other enumerated categories of Art. III, § 2), or is not a "case or controversy" within the meaning of that section; or the cause is not one described by any jurisdictional statute. Our conclusion, that this cause presents no nonjusticiable "political question" settles the only possible doubt that it is a case or controversy. Under the present heading of "Jurisdiction of the Subject Matter" we hold only that the matter set forth in the complaint does arise under the Constitution and is within 28 U.S.C. § 1343.

Article III, § 2 of the Federal Constitution provides that "the judicial Power shall extend to all Cases, in Law and Equity, arising under this Constitution, the Laws of the United States, and Treaties made, or which shall be made, under their Authority; . . ." It is clear that the cause of action is one which "arises under" the Federal Constitution. The complaint alleges that the 1901 statute effects an apportionment that deprives the appellants of the equal protection of the laws in violation of the Fourteenth Amendment. . . .

The appellees refer to *Colegrove* v. *Green,* 328 U.S. 549, as authority that the District Court lacked jurisdiction of the subject matter. Appellees misconceive the holding of that case. The holding was precisely contrary to their reading of it. Seven members of the Court participated in the decision. Unlike many other cases in this field which have assumed without discussion that there was jurisdiction, all three opinions filed in *Colegrove* discussed the question. Two of the opinions expressing the views of four of the Justices, a majority, flatly held that there was jurisdiction of the subject matter. MR. JUSTICE BLACK joined by MR. JUSTICE DOUGLAS and MR. JUSTICE MURPHY stated: "It is my judgment that the District Court had jurisdiction . . . ," citing the predecessor of 28 U.S.C. § 1343 (3), and *Bell* v. *Hood, supra.* 328 U.S., at 568. Mr. Justice Rutledge, writing separately, expressed agreement with this conclusion. . . .

JUSTICIABILITY

In holding that the subject matter of this suit was not justiciable, the District Court relied on *Colegrove* v. *Green, supra,* and subsequent *per curiam* cases. The court stated: "From a review of these decisions there can be no doubt that the federal rule . . . is that the federal courts . . . will not intervene in cases of this type to compel legislative reapportionment." 179 F. Supp., at 826. We understand the District Court to have read the cited cases as compelling the conclusion that since the appellants sought to have a legislative apportionment held unconstitutional, their suit presented a "political question" and was therefore nonjusticiable. We hold that this challenge to an apportionment presents no nonjustciable "political question." The cited cases do not hold the contrary.

Of course the mere fact that the suit seeks protection of a political right does not mean it presents a political question. Such an objection "is little more than a play upon words." *Nixon* v. *Herndon,* 273 U.S. 536, 540. . . .

Our discussion, even at the price of extending this opinion, requires review of a number of political question cases, in order to expose the attributes of the doctrine—attributes which, in various settings, diverge, combine, appear, and disappear in seeming disorderliness. Since that review is undertaken solely to demonstrate that neither singly nor collectively do these cases support a conclusion that this apportionment case is nonjusticiable, we of course do not explore their implications in other contexts. That review reveals that in the Guaranty Clause cases and in the other "political question" cases, it is the relationship between the judiciary and the coordinate branches of the Federal Government, and not the federal judiciary's relationship to the States, which gives rise to the "political question."

We have said that "in determining whether a question falls within [the political question] category, the appropriateness under our system of government of attributing finality to the action of the political departments and also the lack of satisfactory criteria for a judicial determination are dominant considerations." *Coleman* v. *Miller*, 307 U.S. 433, 454-455. The nonjusticiability of a political question is primarily a function of the separation of powers. Much confusion results from the capacity of the "political question" label to obscure the need for case-by-case inquiry. Deciding whether a matter has in any measure been committed by the Constitution to another branch of government, or whether the action of that branch exceeds whatever authority has been committed, is itself a delicate exercise in constitutional interpretation, and is a responsibility of this Court as ultimate interpreter of the Constitution. To demonstrate this requires no less than to analyze representative cases and to infer from them the analytical threads that make up the political question doctrine. We shall then show that none of those threads catches this case. . . .

It is apparent that several formulations which vary slightly according to the settings in which the questions arise may describe a political question, although each has one or more elements which identifies it as essentially a function of the separation of powers. Prominent on the surface of any case held to involve a political question is found a textually demonstrable constitutional commitment of the issue to a coordinate political department; or a lack of judicially discoverable and manageable standards for resolving it; or the impossibility of deciding without an initial policy determination of a kind clearly for nonjudicial discretion; or the impossibility of a court's undertaking independent resolution without expressing lack of the respect due coordinate branches of government; or an unusual need for unquestioning adherence to a political decision already made; or the potentiality of embarrassment from multifarious pronouncements by various departments on one question.

Unless one of these formulations is inextricable from the case at bar, there should be no dismissal for nonjusticiability on the ground of a political question's presence. The doctrine of which we treat is one of "political questions," not of "political cases." The courts cannot reject as "no law suit" a bona fide controversy as to whether some action denominated "political" exceeds constitutional authority. The cases we have reviewed show the necessity for discriminatory inquiry into the precise facts and posture of the particular case, and the impossibility of resolution by any semantic cataloguing.

But it is argued that this case shares the characteristics of decisions that constitute a category not yet considered, cases concerning the Constitution's guaranty in Art. 4, § 4, of a republican form of government. A conclusion as to whether the case at bar does present a political question cannot be confidently reached until we have considered those cases with special care. We shall discover that Guaranty Clause claims involve those elements which define a "political question," and for that reason and no other, they are nonjusticiable. In particular, we shall discover that the nonjusticiability of such claims has nothing to do with their touching upon matters of state governmental organization. . . .

We come, finally to the ultimate inquiry whether our precedents as to what constitutes a nonjusticiable "political question" bring the case before us under the umbrella of that doctrine. A natural beginning is to note whether any of the common characteristics which we have been able to identify and label descriptively are present. We find none: The question here is the consistency of state action with the Federal Constitution. We have no question decided, or to be decided, by a political branch of government coequal with this Court. Nor do we risk embarrassment of our government abroad, or grave disturbance at home if we take issue with Tennessee as to the constitutionality of her action here challenged. Nor need the appellants, in order to succeed in this action, ask the Court to enter upon policy determinations for which judicially manageable standards are lacking. Judicial standards under the Equal Protection Clause are well developed and familiar, and it has been open to courts since the enactment of the Fourteenth Amendment to detemine, if on the particular facts they must, that a discrimination reflects *no* policy, but simply arbitrary and capricious action.

This case does, in one sense, involve the allocation of political power within a State, and the appellants might conceivably have added a claim under the Guaranty Clause. Of course, as we have seen, any reliance on that clause would be futile. But because any reliance on the Guaranty Clause could not have succeeded it does not follow that appellants may not be heard on the equal protection claim which in fact they tender. True, it must be clear that the Fourteenth Amendment claim is not so enmeshed with those political question elements which render Guaranty Clause claims nonjusticiable as actually to present a political question itself. But we have found that not to be the case here. . . .

When challenges to state action respecting matters of "the administration of the affairs of the State and the officers through whom they are conducted" have rested on claims of constitutional deprivation which are amenable to judicial correction, this Court has acted upon its view of the merits of the claim. For example, in *Boyd* v. *Nebraska ex rel. Thayer*, 143 U.S. 135, we reversed the Nebraska Supreme Court's decision that Nebraska's Governor was not a citizen of the United States or of the State and therefore could not continue in office. In *Kennard* v. *Louisiana ex rel. Morgan,* 92 U.S. (2 Otto) 480, and *Foster* v. *Kansas ex rel. Johnston*, 112 U.S. 201, we considered whether persons had been removed from public office by procedures consistent with the Fourteenth Amendment's due process guaranty, and held on the merits that they had. And only last Term, in *Gomillion* v. *Lightfoot*, 364 U.S. 339, we applied the Fifteenth Amendment to strike down a redrafting of municipal boundaries which effected a discriminatory impairment of voting rights, in the face of what a majority of the Court of Appeals thought to be a sweeping commitment to state legislatures of the power to draw and redraw such boundaries.

Gomillion was brought by a Negro, who had been a resident of the City of Tuskegee, Alabama, until the municipal boundaries were so recast by the State Legislature as to exclude practically all Negroes. The plaintiff claimed deprivation of the right to vote in municipal elections. The District Court's dismissal for want of jurisdiction and failure to state a claim upon which relief could be granted was affirmed by the Court of Appeals. This Court unanimously reversed. . . .

We have already noted that the District Court's holding that the subject matter of this complaint was nonjusticiable relied upon *Colegrove* v. *Green, supra,* and later cases. Some of those concerned the choice of members of a state legislature, as in this case; others, like *Colegrove* itself and earlier precedents, *Smiley* v. *Holm,* 285 U.S. 355, *Koenig* v. *Flynn*, 285 U.S. 375, and *Carroll* v. *Becker,* 285 U.S. 380, concerned the choice of Representatives in the Federal Congress. *Smiley, Koenig* and *Carroll* settled the issue in favor of justiciability of questions of congressional redistricting. The Court followed these precedents in *Colegrove* although over the dissent of three of the seven Justices who participated in that decision. On the issue of justiciability, all four Justices comprising a majority relied upon *Smiley* v. *Holm*, but in two opinions, one for three Justices, 328 U.S., at 566, 568, and a separate one by Mr. Justice Rutledge, 328 U.S., at 564. . . .

Article I, §§ 2, 4 and 5 and Amendment XIV, § 2 relate only to congressional elections and obviously do not govern apportionment of state legislatures. However, our decisions in favor of justiciability even in light of those provisions plainly afford no support for the District Court's conclusion that the subject matter of this controversy presents a political question. Indeed, the refusal to award relief in *Colegrove* resulted only from the controlling view of a want of equity. Nor is anything contrary to be found in those *per curiams* that came after *Colegrove*. . . .

We conclude that the complaint's allegations of a denial of equal protection present a justiciable constitutional cause of action upon which appellants are entitled to a trial and a decision. The right asserted is within the reach of judicial protection under the Fourteenth Amendment.

The judgment of the District Court is reversed and the cause is remanded for further proceedings consistent with this opinion.

Reversed and remanded.

Mr. Justice Whittaker did not participate in the decision of this case.

Mr. Justice Douglas, concurring.

While I join the opinion of the Court and, like the Court, do not reach the merits, a word of explanation is necessary. I put to one side the problems of "political" questions involving the distribution of power between this Court, the Congress, and the Chief Executive. We have here a phase of the recurring problem of the relation of the federal courts to state agencies. More particularly, the question is the extent to which a State may weight one person's vote more heavily than it does another's. . . .

There is a third barrier to a State's freedom in prescribing qualifications of voters and that is the Equal Protection Clause of the Fourteenth Amendment, the provision invoked here. And so the question is, may a State weight the vote of one county or one district more heavily than it weights the vote in another?

The traditional test under the Equal Protection Clause has been whether a State has made "an invidious discrimination," as it does when it selects "a particular race or nationality for oppressive treatment." See *Skinner* v. *Oklahoma*, 316 U.S. 535, 541. Universal equality is not the test; there is room for weighting. As we stated in *Williamson* v. *Lee Optical Co.*, 348 U.S. 483, 489, "The prohibition of the Equal Protection Clause goes no further than the invidious discrimination."

I agree with my Brother CLARK that if the allegations in the complaint can be sustained a case for relief is established. We are told that a single vote in Moore County, Tennessee, is worth 19 votes in Hamilton County, that one vote in Stewart or in Chester County is worth nearly eight times a single vote in Shelby or Knox County. The opportunity to prove that an "invidious discrimination" exists should therefore be given the appellants.

It is said that any decision in cases of this kind is beyond the competence of courts. Some make the same point as regards the problem of equal protection in cases involving racial segregation. Yet the legality of claims and conduct is a traditional subject for judicial determination. Adjudication is often perplexing and complicated. An example of the extreme complexity of the task can be seen in a decree apportioning water among the several states. *Nebraska* v. *Wyoming*, 325 U.S. 589, 665. The constitutional guide is often vague, as the decisions under the Due Process and Commerce Clauses show. The problem under the Equal Protection Clause is no more intricate. See Lewis, Legislative Apportionment and the Federal Courts, 71 Harv. L. Rev. 1057, 1083-1084. . . .

As stated by Judge McLaughlin in *Dyer* v. *Kazuhisa Abe,* 138 F. Supp. 220, 236 (an apportionment case in Hawaii which was reversed and dismissed as moot, 256 F. 2d 728):

> The whole thrust of today's legal climate is to end unconstitutional discrimination. It is ludicrous to preclude judicial relief when a mainspring of representative government is impaired. Legislators have no immunity from the Constitution. The legislatures of our land should be made as responsive to the Constitution of the United States as are the citizens who elect the legislators.

With the exceptions of *Colegrove* v. *Green*, 328 U.S. 549; *MacDougall* v. *Green*, 335 U.S. 281; *South* v. *Peters*, 339 U.S. 276, and the decisions they spawned, the Court has never thought that protection of voting rights was beyond judicial cognizance. Today's treatment of those cases removes the only impediment to judicial cognizance of the claims stated in the present complaint.

The justiciability of the present claims being established, any relief accorded can be fashioned in the light of well-known principles of equity.

Mr. Justice Clark, concurring.

One emerging from the rash of opinions with their accompanying clashing of views may well find himself suffering a mental blindness. The Court holds that the appellants have alleged a cause of action. However, it refuses to award relief here—although the facts are undisputed—and fails to give the District Court any guidance whatever. One dissenting opinion, bursting with words that go through so much and conclude with so little, contemns the majority action as "a massive repudiation of the experience of our whole past." Another describes the complaint as merely asserting conclusory allegations that Tennessee's apportionment is "incorrect," "arbitrary," "obsolete," and "unconstitutional." I believe it can be shown that this case is distinguishable from earlier cases dealing with the distribution of political power by a State, that a patent violation of the Equal Protection Clause of the United States Constitution has been shown, and that an appropriate remedy may be formulated. . . .

The controlling facts cannot be disputed. It appears from the record that 37 percent of the voters of Tennessee elect 20 of the 33 Senators while 40 percent of the voters elect 63 of the 99 members of the House. But this might not on its face be an "invidious discrimination," *Williamson* v. *Lee Optical of Oklahoma*, 348 U.S. 483, 489 (1955), for a "statutory discrimination will not be set aside if any state of facts reasonably may be conceived to justify it." *McGowan* v. *Maryland*, 366 U.S. 420, 426 (1961).

It is true that the apportionment policy incorporated in Tennessee's Constitution, i.e., state-wide numerical equality of representation with certain minor qualifications, is a rational one. On a county-by-county comparison a districting plan based thereon naturally will have disparities in representation due to the qualifications. But this to my mind does not raise constitutional problems, for the overall policy is reasonable. However, the root of the trouble is not in Tennessee's Constitution, for admittedly its policy has not been followed. The discrimination lies in the action of Tennessee's Assembly in allocating legislative seats to counties or districts created by it. Try as one may, Tennessee's apportionment just cannot be made to fit the pattern cut by its Constitution. This was the finding of the District Court. The policy of the Constitution referred to by the dissenters, therefore, is of no relevance here. We must examine what the Assembly has done. The frequency and magnitude of the inequalities in the present districting admit of no policy whatever. An examination of Table 1 accompanying this opinion conclusively reveals that the apportionment picture in Tennessee is a topsy-turvical of gigantic proportions. This is not to say that some of the disparity cannot be explained, but when the entire Table is examined—comparing the voting strength of counties of like population as well as contrasting that of the smaller with the larger counties—it leaves but one conclusion, namely that Tennessee's apportionment is a crazy quilt without rational basis. At the risk of being accused of picking out a few of the horribles I shall allude to a series of examples that are taken from Table 1.

As is admitted there is a wide disparity of voting strength between the large and small counties. Some samples are: Moore County has a total representation of two with a population (2,340) of only one-eleventh of Rutherford County (25,316) with the same representation; Decatur County (5,563) has the same representation as Carter (23,303) though the latter has four times the population; likewise, Loudon County (13,264), Houston (3,084), and Anderson County (33,990) have the same representation, i.e., 1.25 each. But it is said that in this illustration all of the underrepresented counties contain municipalities of over 10,000 population and they therefore should be included under the "urban" classification, rationalizing this disparity as an attempt to effect a rural-urban political balance. But in so doing one is caught up in the backlash of his own bull whip, for many counties have no municipalities with a population exceeding 10,000, yet the same invidious discrimination is present. For example:

County	Population	Representation
Carter	23,303	1.10
Maury	24,556	2.25
Washington	36,967	1.93
Madison	37,245	3.50

Likewise, counties with no municipality of over 10,000 suffer a similar discrimination:

County	Population	Representation
Grundy	6,540	0.95
Chester	6,391	2.00
Cumberland	9,593	0.63
Crockett	9,676	2.00
Loudon	13,264	1.25
Fayette	13,577	2.50

This could not be an effort to give political balance between rural and urban populations. Since discrimination is present among counties of like population, the plan is neither consistent nor rational. It discriminates horizontally creating gross disparities between rural areas themselves as well as between urban areas themselves, still maintaining the wide vertical disparity already pointed out between rural and urban. . . .

The truth is that—although this case has been here for two years and has had over six hours' argument (three times the ordinary case) and has been most carefully considered over and over again by us in Conference and individually—no one, not even the State nor the dissenters, has come up with any rational basis for Tennessee's apportionment statute.

No one—except the dissenters advocating the HARLAN "adjusted 'total representation' " formula—contends that mathematical equality among voters is required by the Equal Protection Clause. But certainly there must be some rational design to a State's districting. The discrimination here does not fit any pattern—as I have said, it is but a crazy quilt. My Brother HARLAN contends that other proposed apportionment plans contain disparities. Instead of chasing those rabbits he should first pause long enough to meet appellants proof of discrimination by showing that in fact the present plan follows a rational policy. Not being able to do this, he merely counters with such generalities as "classic legislative judgment," no "significant discrepancy," and "de minimis departures." I submit that even a casual glance at the present apportionment picture shows these conclusions to be entirely fanciful. If present representation has a policy at all, it is to maintain the status quo of invidious discrimination at any cost. Like the District Court, I conclude that appellants have met the burden of showing "Tennessee is guilty of a clear violation of the state constitution and of the [federal] rights of the plaintiffs. . . ."

Although I find the Tennessee apportionment statute offends the Equal Protection Clause, I would not consider intervention by this Court into so delicate a field if there were any other relief available to the people of Tennessee. But the majority of the people of Tennessee have no "practical opportunities for exerting their political weight at the polls" to correct the existing "invidious discrimination." Tennessee has no initiative and referendum. I have searched diligently for other "practical opportunities" present under the law. I find none other than through the federal courts. The majority of the voters have been caught up in a legislative strait jacket. Tennessee has an "informed, civically militant electorate" and "an aroused popular conscience," but it does not sear "the conscience of the people's representatives." This is because the legislative policy has riveted the present seats in the Assembly to their respective constituencies, and by the votes of their incumbents a reapportionment of any kind is prevented. The people have been rebuffed at the hands of the Assembly; they have tried the constitutional convention route, but since the call must originate in the Assembly it, too, has been fruitless. They have tried Tennessee courts with the same result, and Governors have fought the tide only to flounder. It is said that there is recourse in Congress and perhaps that may be, but from a practical standpoint this is without substance. To date Congress has never undertaken such a task in any State. We therefore must conclude that the people of Tennessee are stymied and without judicial intervention will be saddled with the present discrimination in the affairs of their state government.

Finally, we must consider if there are any appropriate modes of effective judicial relief. The federal courts are, of course, not forums for political debate, nor should they resolve themselves into state constitutional conventions or legislative assemblies. Nor should their jurisdiction be exercised in the hope that such a declaration, as is made today, may have the direct effect of bringing on legislative action and relieving the courts of the problem of fashioning relief. To my mind this would be nothing less than blackjacking the Assembly into reapportioning the State. If judicial competence were lacking to fashion an effective decree, I would dismiss this appeal. However, like the Solicitor General of the United States, I see no such difficulty in the position of this case. One plan might be to start with the existing assembly districts, consolidate some of them, and award the seats thus released to those counties suffering the most egregious discrimination. Other possibilities are present and might be more effective. But the plan here suggested would at least release the strangle hold now on the Assembly and permit it to redistrict itself. . . .

As John Rutledge (later Chief Justice) said 175 years ago in the course of the Constitutional Convention, a chief function of the Court is to secure the national rights. Its decision today supports the proposition for which our forebears fought and many died, namely that "to be fully conformable to the principle of right, the form of government must be representative." That is the keystone upon which our government was founded and lacking which no republic can survive. It is well for this Court to practice self-restraint and discipline in constitutional adjudication, but never in its history have those principles received sanction where the national rights of so many have been so clearly infringed for so long a time. National respect for the courts is more enhanced through the forthright enforcement of those rights rather than by rendering them nugatory through the interposition of subterfuges. In my view the ultimate decision today is in the greatest tradition of this Court.

Mr. Justice Stewart, concurring.

The separate writings of my dissenting and concurring Brothers stray so far from the subject of today's decision as to convey, I think, a distressingly inaccurate impression of what the Court decides. For that reason, I think it appropriate, in joining the opinion of the Court, to emphasize in a few words what the opinion does and does not say.

The Court today decides three things and no more: "(a) that the court possessed jurisdiction of the subject matter; (b) that a justiciable cause of action is stated upon which appellants would be entitled to appropriate relief; and (c) . . . that the appellants have standing to challenge the Tennessee apportionment statutes."

The complaint in this case asserts that Tennessee's system of apportionment is utterly arbitrary—without any possible justification in rationality. The District Court did not reach the merits of that claim, and this Court quite properly expresses no view on the subject. Contrary to the suggestion of my Brother HARLAN, the Court does not say or imply that "state legislatures must be so structured as to reflect with approximate equality the voice of every voter." The Court does not say or imply that there is anything in the Federal Constitution "to prevent a State, acting not irrationally, from choosing any electoral legislative structure it thinks best suited to the interests, temper, and customs of its people." And contrary to the suggestion of my Brother DOUGLAS, the Court most assuredly does not decide the question, "may a State weight the vote of one county or one district more heavily than it weights the vote in another?"

In *MacDougall* v. *Green,* 335 U.S. 281, the Court held that the Equal Protection Clause does not "deny a State the power to assure a proper diffusion of political initiative as between its thinly populated counties and those having concentrated masses, in view of the fact that the latter have practical opportunities for exerting their political weight at the polls not available to the former." 335 U.S., at 284. In case after case arising under the Equal Protection Clause the Court has said what it said again only last Term—that "the Fourteenth Amendment permits the States a wide scope of discretion in enacting laws which affect some groups of citizens differently than others." *McGowan* v. *Maryland,* 336 U.S. 420, 425. In case after case arising under that Clause we have also said that "the burden of establishing the unconstitutionality of a statute rests on him who assails it." *Metropolitan Casualty Ins. Co.* v. *Brownell,* 294 U.S. 580, 584.

Today's decision does not turn its back on these settled precedents. I repeat, the Court today decides only: (1) that the District Court possessed jurisdiction of the subject matter; (2) that the complaint presents a justiciable controversy; (3) that the appellants have standing. My Brother CLARK has made a convincing prima facie showing that Tennessee's system of apportionment is in fact utterly arbitrary—without any possible justification in rationality. My Brother HARLAN has, with imagination and ingenuity, hypothesized possibly rational bases for Tennessee's system. But the merits of this case are not before us now. The defendants have not yet had an opportunity to be heard in defense of the State's system of apportionment; indeed, they have not yet even filed an answer to the complaint. As in other cases, the proper place for the trial is in the trial court, not here.

Mr. Justice Frankfurter, whom Mr. Justice Harlan joins, dissenting.

The Court today reverses a uniform course of decision established by a dozen cases, including one by which the very claim now sustained was unanimously rejected only five years ago. The impressive body of rulings thus cast aside reflected the equally uniform course of our political history regarding the relationship between population and legislative representation—a wholly different matter from denial of the franchise to individuals because of race, color, religion or sex. Such a massive repudiation of the experience of our whole past in asserting destructively novel judicial power demands a detailed analysis of the role of this Court in our constitutional scheme. Disregard of inherent limits in the effective exercise of the Court's "judicial Power" not only presages the futility of judicial intervention in the essentially political conflict of forces by which the relation between population and representation has time out of mind been and now is determined. It may well impair the Court's position as the ultimate organ of "the supreme Law of the Land" in that vast range of legal problems, often strongly entangled in popular feeling, on which this Court must pronounce. The Court's authority—possessed neither of the purse nor the sword—ultimately rests on sustained public confidence in its moral sanction. Such feeling must be nourished by the Court's complete detachment, in fact and in appearance, from political entanglements and by abstention from injecting itself into the clash of political forces in political settlements.

A hypothetical claim resting on abstract assumptions is now for the first time made the basis for affording illusory relief for a particular evil even though it foreshadows deeper and more pervasive difficulties in consequence. The claim is hypothetical and the assumptions are abstract because the Court does not vouchsafe the lower courts—state and federal—guide-lines for formulating specific, definite, wholly unprecedented remedies for the inevitable litigations that today's umbrageous disposition is bound to stimulate in connection with politically motivated reapportionments in so many States. In such a setting, to promulgate jurisdiction in the abstract is meaningless. It is devoid of reality as "a brooding omnipresence in the sky" for it conveys no intimation what relief, if any, a District Court is capable of affording that would not invite legislatures to play ducks and drakes with the judiciary. For this Court to direct the District Court to enforce a claim to which the Court has over the years consistently found itself required to deny legal enforcement and at the same time to find it necessary to withhold any guidance to the lower court how to enforce this turnabout, new legal claim, manifests an odd—indeed an esoteric—conception of judicial propriety. One of the Court's supporting opinions, as elucidated by commentary, unwittingly affords a disheartening preview of the mathematical quagmire (apart from divers judicially inappropriate and elusive determinants), into which this Court today catapults the lower courts of the country without so much as adumbrating the basis for a legal calculus as a means of extrication. Even assuming the indispensable intellectual disinterestedness on the part of judges in such matters, they do not have accepted legal standards or criteria or even reliable analogies to draw upon for making judicial judgments. To charge courts with the task of accommodating the incommensurable factors of policy that underlie these mathematical puzzles is to attribute, however flatteringly, omnicompetence to judges. The Framers of the Constitution persistently rejected a proposal that embodied this assumption and Thomas Jefferson never entertained it.

Recent legislation, creating a district appropriately described as "an atrocity of ingenuity," is not unique. Considering the gross inequality among legislative electoral units within almost every State, the Court naturally shrinks from asserting that in districting at least substantial equality is a constitutional requirement enforceable by courts. Room continues to be allowed for weighting. This of course implies that geography, economics, urban-rural conflict, and all the other non-legal factors which have throughout our history entered into political districting are to some extent not to be ruled out in the undefined vista now opened up by review in the federal courts of state reapportionments. To some extent—aye, there's the rub. In effect, today's decision empowers the courts of the country to devise what should constitute the proper composition of the legislatures of the fifty States. If state courts should for one reason or another find themselves unable to discharge this task, the duty of doing so is put on the federal courts or on this Court, if State views do not satisfy this Court's notion of what is proper districting.

We were soothingly told at the bar of this Court that we need not worry about the kind of remedy a court could effectively fashion once the abstract constitutional right to have courts pass on a state-wide system of electoral districting is recognized as a matter of judicial rhetoric, because legislatures would heed the Court's admonition. This is not only an euphoric hope. It implies a sorry confession of judicial impotence in place of a frank acknowledgment that there is not under our Constitution a judicial remedy for every political mischief, for every undesirable exerise of legislative power. The Framers carefully and with deliberate forethought refused so to enthrone the judiciary. In this situation, as in others of like nature, appeal for relief does not belong here. Appeal must be to an informed, civically militant electorate. In a democratic society like ours, relief must come through an aroused popular conscience that sears the conscience of the people's representatives. In any event there is nothing judicially more unseemly nor more self-defeating than for this Court to make *in terrorem* pronouncements, to indulge in merely empty rhetoric, sounding a word of promise to the ear, sure to be disappointing to the hope. . . .

In sustaining appellants' claim, based on the Fourteenth Amendment, that the District Court may entertain this suit, this Court's uniform course of decision over the years are overruled or disregarded. Explicitly it begins with *Colegrove* v. *Green, supra,* decided in 1946, but its roots run deep in the Court's historic adjudicatory process.

Colegrove held that a federal court should not entertain an action for declaratory and injunctive relief to adjudicate the constitutionality, under the Equal Protection Clause and other federal constitutional and statutory provisions, of a state statute establishing the respective districts for the State's election of Representatives to the Congress. Two opinions were written by the four Justices who composed the majority of the seven sitting members of the Court. Both opinions joining in the result in *Colegrove* v. *Green* agreed that considerations were controlling which dictated denial of jurisdiction though not in the strict sense of want of power. While the two opinions show a divergence of view regarding some of these considerations, there are important points of concurrence. Both opinions demonstrate a predominant concern, first, with avoiding federal judicial involvement in matters traditionally left to legislative policy-making; second, with respect to the difficulty—in view of the nature of the problems of apportionment and its history in this country—of drawing on or devising judicial standards for judgment, as opposed to legislative determinations, of the part which mere numerical equality among voters should play as a criterion for the allocation of political power; and, third, with problems of finding appropriate modes of relief—particularly, the problem of resolving the essentially political issue of the relative merits of at-large elections and elections held in districts of unequal population.

The broad applicability of these considerations—summarized in the loose shorthand phrase, "political question"—in cases involving a State's apportionment of voting power among its numerous localities has led the Court, since 1946, to recognize their controlling effect in a variety of situations. . . .

The present case involves all of the elements that have made the Guarantee Clause cases nonjusticiable. It is, in effect, a Guarantee Clause claim masquerading under a different label. But it cannot make the case more fit for judicial action that appellants invoke the Fourteenth Amendment rather than Art. IV. § 4, where, in fact, the gist of their complaint is the same—unless it can be found that the Fourteenth Amendment speaks with greater particularity to their situation. We have been admonished to avoid "the tyranny of labels." *Snyder* v. *Massachusetts,* 291, U.S. 97, 114. Art. IV, § 4, is not committed by express constitutional terms to Congress. It is the nature of the controversies arising under it, nothing else, which has made it judicially unenforceable. . . .

What, then, is this question of legislative apportionment? Appellants invoke the right to vote and to have their votes counted. But they are permitted to vote and their votes are counted. They go to the polls, they cast their ballots, they send their representatives to the state councils. Their complaint is simply that the representatives are not sufficiently numerous or powerful—in short, that Tennessee has adopted a basis of representation with which they are dissatisfied. Talk of "debasement" or "dilution" is circular talk. One cannot speak of "debasement" or "dilution" of the value of a vote until there is first defined a standard of reference as to what a vote should be worth. What is actually asked of the Court in this case is to choose among competing bases of representation—ultimately, really, among competing theories of political philosophy—

in order to establish an appropriate frame of government for the State of Tennessee and thereby for all the States of the Union. . . .

The notion that representation proportioned to the geographic spread of population is so universally accepted as a necessary element of equality between man and man that it must be taken to be the standard of a political equality preserved by the Fourteenth Amendment—that it is, in appellants' words "the basic principle of representative government"—is, to put it bluntly, not true. However desirable and however desired by some among the great political thinkers and framers of our government, it has never been generally practiced, today or in the past. It was not the English system, it was not the colonial system, it was not the system chosen for the national government by the Constitution, it was not the system exclusively or even predominantly practiced by the States at the time of adoption of the Fourteenth Amendment, it is not predominantly practiced by the States today. Unless judges, the judges of this Court, are to make their private views of political wisdom the measure of the Constitution—views which in all honesty cannot but give the appearance, if not reflect the reality, of involvement with the business of partisan politics so inescapably a part of apportionment controversies—the Fourteenth Amendment, "itself a historical product," *Jackman* v. *Rosenbaum Co.,* 260 U.S. 22, 31, provides no guide for judicial oversight of the representation problem. . . .

Contemporary apportionment. Detailed recent studies are available to describe the present-day constitutional and statutory status of apportionment in the fifty States. They demonstrate a decided twentieth-century trend away from population as the exclusive base of representation. Today, only a dozen state constitutions provide for periodic legislative reapportionment of both houses by a substantially unqualified application of the population standard, and only about a dozen more prescribe such reapportionment for even a single chamber. "Specific provision for county representation in at least one house of the state legislature has been increasingly adopted since the end of the 19th century. . . ." More than twenty States now guarantee each county at least one seat in one of their houses regardless of population, and in nine others county or town units are given equal representation in one legislative branch, whatever the number of each unit's inhabitants. Of course, numerically considered, "These provisions invariably result in overrepresentation of the least populated areas. . . ." And in an effort to curb the political dominance of metropolitan regions, at least ten States now limit the maximum entitlement of any single county (or, in some cases, city) in one legislative house—another source of substantial numerical disproportion.

Moreover, it is common knowledge that the legislatures have not kept reapportionment up to date, even where state constitutions in terms require it. In particular, the pattern of according greater per capita representation to rural, relatively sparsely populated areas—the same pattern which finds expression in various state constitutional provisions, and which has been given effect in England and elsewhere—has, in some of the States been made the law by legislative inaction in the face of population shifts. Throughout the country, urban and suburban areas tend to be given higher representation ratios than do rural areas.

The stark fact is that if among the numerous widely varying principles and practices that control state legislative apportionment today there is any generally prevailing feature, that feature is geographic inequality in relation to the population standard. Examples could be endlessly multiplied. . . .

Manifestly, the Equal Protection Clause supplies no clearer guide for judicial examination of apportionment methods than would the Guarantee Clause itself. Apportionment, by its character, is a subject of extraordinary complexity, involving—even after the fundamental theoretical issues concerning what is to be represented in a representative legislature have been fought out or compromised—considerations of geography, demography, electoral convenience, economic and social cohesions or divergencies among particular local groups, communications, the practical effects of political institutions like the lobby and the city machine, ancient traditions and ties of settled usage, respect for proven incumbents of long experience and senior status, mathematical mechanics, censuses compiling relevant data, and a host of others. Legislative responses throughout the country to the reapportionment demands of the 1960 Census have glaringly confirmed that these are not factors that lend themselves to evaluations of a nature that are the staple of judicial determinations or for which judges are equipped to adjudicate by legal training or experience or native wit. And this is the more so true because in every strand of this complicated, intricate web of values meet the contending forces of partisan politics. The practical significance of apportionment is that the next election results may differ because of it. Apportionment battles are overwhelmingly party or intra-party contests. It will add a virulent source of friction and tension in federal-state relations to embroil the federal judiciary in them. . . .

PART III

The Impact of Baker v. Carr

☆ 8 ☆

JUDICIAL USURPATION AND DESTRUCTION OF OUR FEDERAL SYSTEM

The Baker v. Carr decision evoked a storm of criticism from state officials, particularly legislators, who viewed it as judicial usurpation of their prerogatives, and by status quo interests, which perceived the decision as a threat to their political power. Immediately an effort was launched to abrogate Baker by amending the Constitution. At the Sixteenth Assembly of the States (a biennial meeting of state officials, two-thirds legislators, sponsored by the Council of State Governments) in December, 1962, the executive director of COSGO urged a counter attack and the Assembly responded by passage of the following resolution.

Proposed Amendment to the Constitution

A (Joint) Resolution

Memorializing Congress to call a convention for the purpose of proposing an amendment to the Constitution of the United States.

Resolved by the House of Representatives, the Senate concurring, that this Legislature respectfully petitions the Congress of the United States to call a convention for the purpose of proposing the following article as an amendment to the Constitution of the United States.

From *State Government,* Winter, 1963, pp. 12–13, 32.

"ARTICLE—

"Section 1. No provision of this Constitution, or any amendment thereto, shall restrict or limit any state in the apportionment of representation in its legislature.

"Section 2. The judicial power of the United States shall not extend to any suit in law or equity, or to any controversy, relating to apportionment of representation in a state legislature.

"Section 3. This article shall be inoperative unless it shall have been ratified as an amendment to the Constitution by the Legislatures of three-fourths of the several States within seven years from the date of its submission."

Be it Further Resolved that if Congress shall have proposed an amendment to the Constitution identical with that contained in this resolution prior to January 1, 1965, this application for a convention shall no longer be of any force or effect.

Be It Further Resolved that a duly attested copy of this resolution be immediately transmitted to the Secretary of the Senate of the United States, the Clerk of the House of Representatives of the United States and to each member of the Congress from this State.

Speaker-Elect Robert D. Hasse of Wisconsin spoke in support of the resolution. States must be reapportioned fairly, he said, but it had even been suggested that federal courts have the right to find state constitutions themselves unconstitutional. Not merely reapportionment is involved, he emphasized, but basic rights. He felt that nothing short of the means suggested in the resolution at hand would stop the federal government from interfering in reapportionment. The resolution, he summarized, would tell the federal government it no longer has any jurisdiction in reapportionment.

Senator King of Ohio spoke in opposition. He suggested that an effort was being made to rewrite the Constitution of the United States, and hurriedly. He reported that the resolution in question was arrived at in the last hour of the committee's meeting, and asserted that it goes the whole way to throw the federal government out of any role in apportionment. It was a shameful thing, he added, to deny the people the protection of equal rights under the Fourteenth Amendment of the United States Constitution.

Discussion from the floor led, by unanimous consent, to a slight change in punctuation at one point in the resolution, for clarification (incorporated in the text above). Following the discussion, the resolution was submitted for vote. The delegations caucused, then approved it by vote of 26 to 10, with 10 passing.

Statement of the Executive Director of the Council of State Governments[1]

On May 26, 1962, the United States Supreme Court ruled in the case of *Baker* v. *Carr* that federal courts could take jurisdiction over the question of state apportionment policies. The judicial restraint counselled by Justice Frankfurter was not observed. The same eminent jurist's advice to his brethren that they avoid "involvement with the business of partisan politics so inescapably a part of apportionment controversies" also was ignored. The Supreme Court has planted both feet in the political jungle. To me, the only surprising facet of *Baker* v. *Carr* and its aftermath is the relish with which some federal courts have wielded their now-declared power to tell the states what they shall do—or else. In the few short months since the decision, there has been enough litigation to confuse the situation for years. And the end is not in sight, even as a glimmer.

What can be done? We can wait, wring our hands and hope that subsequent Supreme Court determination of specific issues, as yet unresolved by *Baker* v. *Carr,* will perhaps leave some small area within which the states can retain authority over basic apportionment policies. Or we can decide to take a stand, utilizing the constitutional authority vested in the states by Article V. As I said earlier, the states *can* hope to initiate an appropriate amendment which would put reasonable limitations on this type of federal judicial intervention. But it must be in such form as to gain truly widespread support, and the states must be prepared to take greater initiative in implementing their own constitutional provisions relative to reapportionment.

[1] From the annual report to the Board of Managers.

☆ 9 ☆

A MILESTONE OF LIBERTY AND PROGRESS

National Civic Review Editorial

In sharp contrast to the preceding expressions of state officialdom is this editorial in the organ of the National Municipal League, a reform association which since about 1900 has had a profound impact on city government by its promotion of the council-manager plan, nonpartisan elections, civil service, municipal home rule, and city planning. Reapportionment is a major concern of the League, which regards urban underrepresentation in legislatures as a paramount handicap of municipal government. An excellent source of current developments is the "Representation" section of its monthly Review.

In considering important consequences of the impact of this reapportionment decision there is another "plus" which will mean a lot to the country. *Baker* v. *Carr* has triggered more discussion of the basic principles upon which our representative form of government is based than our country has witnessed for many years. At the time of the founding of our nation the great men of the day explored these fundamental principles quite thoroughly. They were also discussed extensively throughout the nation when our federal constitution was ratified. The general public then knew

"Consequences of Decision," *National Civic Review,* October, 1962, p. 481. Reprinted by permission.

the principles back of our triple layer form of government because of this public dialogue. Now due to the winds of reform created by reapportionment actions there is a great revisit to history by students of political science, politicians and ordinary citizens interested in the future of our nation.

As the first five months of activity are evaluated, it is well to take a look at the nationwide consequences of *Baker* v. *Carr*. My analysis is:

1. The people know they need no longer suffer from archaic unrepresentative state government.
2. State legislatures know that unless they reapportion themselves fairly the courts will do so.
3. Reapportioned state governments will become more effective parts of our governmental machinery.
4. The oft-repeated words "states' rights" will now assume real meaning as states begin again to exercise their governmental powers.
5. Unshackling of long-dormant state powers will enable urban problems to be dealt with at state capitals with lessened reliance upon Washington.
6. Cities after decades of denials and frustrations will have the votes to secure essential home rule powers to meet local needs.
7. It is certain that archaic state legislative machinery will now be modernized.
8. Genuine state constitutional reform is now possible.
9. The extensive nation-wide dialogue on the fundamentals of our system of government provides an opportunity to restudy and reallocate public powers and functions to those levels of government best able to perform them under twentieth-century conditions.
10. Even the doubters who depreciated the effectiveness of court jurisdiction must now concede it has been dramatically effective.

☆ 10 ☆

THE PROGENY OF BAKER v. CARR

Charles S. Rhyne

The welter of litigation following the Baker *case is surveyed in this article, especially prepared for this book by the General Counsel of the National Association of Municipal Law Officers. The author, a past president of the American Bar Association, was one of the (successful) attorneys in the* Baker *case. He keeps an eagle eye on developments in this area on behalf of the NAMLA. His article points up the numerous issues which the Supreme Court must decide, sooner or later, as a consequence of venturing into this "political thicket."*

Baker v. *Carr* has had, and is having, a cataclysmic impact on legislative apportionment. By any yardstick of measurement that decision must be ranked with the more significant Supreme Court pronouncements dealing with government and the constitutional requirement of equality of individuals. *Baker* v. *Carr*'s impact can perhaps best be presented viewed negatively. For instance, in only eight states has there been, subsequent to *Baker* v. *Carr,* no major judicial, legislative, or constitutional action on the reapportionment issue (Alaska, Arizona, Arkansas, Minnesota, Montana, South Carolina and South Dakota). But in some of these states reapportionment had been carried out not too long before March, 1962, the date on which *Baker* v. *Carr* was decided.

A Brief Refresher in History

To put the discussion into proper perspective, it is well to recall a few basic facts about the malapportionment picture. *Baker* v. *Carr* involved facts showing that one-third of the people in Tennessee controlled two-thirds of the legislature. One rural vote was worth twenty urban votes. Tennessee had not been reapportioned since 1901, and then it had not been done strictly on a population standard. The U.S. Supreme Court was told that 27 states had not been reapportioned in the past 25 years and 8 states in over 50 years. Yet, four-fifths of the state constitutions require reapportionment every ten years on the basis of population or number of voters. Others, which give one representative to each county or town, were adopted when those units were substantially equal in population. Basic state constitutional and statutory provisions for reapportionment are often so ancient as to be out of place in today's urban society.

State government is by far the most antiquated part of the governmental machinery in our nation. And the picture has grown worse as ever accelerating urbanization has increased. Pressing problems arising from this growing metropolitan population are not being met by the states due to rural control of legislatures. As city growth has mushroomed, urban votes, as compared with rural votes, are devalued from two to one to one-thousand to one (Vermont). This situation has led to such cynicism and loss of confidence in so many state governments that they have really forfeited any respectful place in our governmental scheme. Up to *Baker* v. *Carr,* prospects for a change in this government by minority were almost nil.

The Decision Itself

A few words of essential background about this landmark decision are also in order. The Supreme Court's decision established three things:

1. Individual voters have court standing to sue to prevent dilution of their voting rights;
2. Courts must consider such a voter claim and grant relief if it is well founded in fact;
3. Such court protection of voting rights raises a question of constitutional right rather than a "political question."

Supreme Court justices wrote five separate opinions explaining the Tennessee decision and the dissents. Basically, the Court decided that when a state creates the right to vote, that right cannot be then apportioned in fractional part to city voters and in magnified measure to rural voters. The Court recognized that when votes are rendered so unequal by dilution as to be ineffective, they are effectively denied.

"Political Thicket" Cliché Rejected

The Court brushed aside the "political thicket" cliché and unfrocked gross malapportionment as "invidious discrimination" in violation of the Fourteenth Amendment. It thus cleared up confusion and swept away unfortunate misconceptions created in 1946 when the minority opinion in *Colgrove* v. *Green,* authored by Mr. Justice Frankfurter, called apportionment by state legislation a "political thicket" and urged that it was "off limits" for the federal courts. Only two justices agreed with the Frankfurter cliché then; it never achieved the status of a decision of the Court. But so clever was the phrase that from 1946 to 1962 the courts had merely cited the cliché and denied court protection to voter rights in this field. The Court thus turned away from decision by cliché or slogan to decision on the facts of each case.

The power exercised by the Court in asserting jurisdiction to end malapportionment is, therefore, the ancient and well-defined power and duty of the courts to provide relief against denial of constitutional rights. The ultimate reason courts exist is to protect and enforce constitutional rights. And this is true of both state and federal courts. Without court protection the constitutional rights of citizens, even though spelled out in exact words in the constitution, are worthless. Communist Russia has proved this.

The Supreme Court held than courts may not decline to exercise their powers to protect the right to vote when that right of certain urban voters is being purposely diluted. That the guarantee of equal protection of the laws contained in the Fourteenth Amendment stands as a ban against invidious discrimination by state law against any voter is now settled.

What the Courts Have Said

A short analysis of what the courts have said and done since *Baker* v. *Carr* is difficult, but the major actions are as follows:

1. Immediate relief has always been withheld by the courts to give the legislature a fair chance to correct existing evils.
2. Legislatures generally take advantage of the opportuniity thus provided to reapportion, even though their end product does not always come up to court requirements. This means some legislatures may have to make several attempts at the problem (for instance, Wisconsin, Florida, Georgia, and Mississippi) before solving it equitably.
3. While legislatures might not like the law as laid down by the courts, there has been no real clash between the courts and legislatures.
4. Existing laws have sometimes been invalidated and legislatures ordered by the courts to adopt valid laws by a fixed deadline under threat of court action unless proper legislative action is forthcoming. And if such legislative action is not forthcoming, the courts have reapportioned the legislature by judicial decree.
5. Many courts have recognized that the equality requirements of the Fourteenth Amendment require apportionment of both houses of a state legislature on the basis of population, but some tribunals have upheld an apportioning scheme where one house is based on population and the other on a standard other than population.
6. While some courts complain that no clear definition of what constitutes "individious discrimination" has yet been laid down by

the U.S. Supreme Court, there has actually been relatively little difficulty in applying that standard on a one man-one vote basis.

"Little Federal Plan"

The apportioning of one house on a geographical basis is a practice the Supreme Court has not yet definitely adjudicated, so it is being raised in many pending cases. This contention is based on the claim that in states with scattered and sparse populations this is a "fair" way to provide representation, and that since one house of Congress is based on the equality of man and the other on equality of states, such a plan is equally applicable to representation in state legislature. Colorado and Nebraska voters adopted such plans on November 6, 1962, and Oregon voters rejected the idea. In every court case this is the rural politicians' first line of defense, but the analogy to federalism is misleading and false. The equality required by the Fourteenth Amendment is equality of people, not geography. And the manner of representation for Congress is based on the underlying rationale that the United States was originally a federation of independent sovereignties. But a state is not a federation of counties and other political subdivisions. The equality of man provision of the Fourteenth Amendment does expressly apply to all state laws, including those fixing representation in state legislatures. The U.S. Supreme Court, sooner or later, will refuse to sustain unjust urban-voter discrimination on the basis of this so-called "little federal plan."

The "Invidious Discrimination" Standard

Much has been written about the "invidious discrimination" standard expressed in *Baker* v. *Carr* by those seeking exact guidelines for decision of cases. Actually, the standard is as clear and concise as other standards commonly utilized in American jurisprudence. Standards such as the "reasonable man" in tort liability litigation, the "prudent man" in business law, "public interest, convenience and necessity" in public utility law and many others that could be mentioned have worked well. Courts and juries constantly test facts against these standards to determine who wins and who loses lawsuits. The "invidious discrimination" standard should give little difficulty. Actually the courts are having no trouble with this and the equally clear "equality" standard.

The One Man-One Vote Principle

The "one man-one vote" principle must prevail in the area of state legislative apportionment to satisfy the requirements of the Fourteenth Amendment. In the *Wesberry* v. *Sanders* case, the Supreme Court held that the Constitution requires the one man-one vote principle in forming districts for electing representatives in Congress, and the application of this democratic tenet should be extended to legislative apportionment on the state and local levels as well. Ours is a government of the people, with tremendous problems and needs which only they can solve and satisfy, acting cooperatively under our representative form of government. The people must be given the right to govern themselves in accordance with the will of the majority. The problems of modern-day state governments will not be solved by the creation of legislative impasses which result where one house of a state legislature is elected on a population basis and the other elected on a standard other than population. By according to the majority the full vitality of its voting franchise in the state legislatures, the Supreme Court will not have deprived the minority of a legislative forum in which to express its views. The minority can be adequately represented without investing it with a veto power over the majority. A full vote should not be dependent upon where a man lives, the color of his skin, his religion, or national origin.

A State Referendum May Not Nullify the Requirements of the Fourteenth Amendment

When the voters have been afforded a choice between reapportionment plans based upon population and other systems, a rejection of a population-oriented plan should not be germane in determining whether invidious discrimination exists in violation of the Fourteenth Amendment. The courts cannot know whether the defeat of a plan calling for fair apportionment was brought about because the majority did not desire equal apportionment or whether the opponents of equal apportionment were better organized; or whether the voters were not given a clear choice between apportionment based upon population and the malapportioned plan approved. In any event, it has been judicially stated that "the inalienable constitutional right of equal protection cannot be made to depend upon the will of the majority" (*Thigpen* v. *Meyers*, 211 F. Supp. 826, 832 [W. D. Wash. 1962]).

Baker v. *Carr* reasserts the right to vote as the most basic right of Americans. Voting is the heart of our governmental process—our great trademark. So is equality. The great principle of equality cannot be denied to voters without destroying the spirit, the purpose, and the very terms of our Constitution and the Declaration of Independence. When the principle of equality is enforced, discrimination ends. When the Supreme Court finally enunciates the one man-one vote principle as applicable to all state and local voting, *Baker* v. *Carr* will have fulfilled its role as the Magna Carta of the elector.

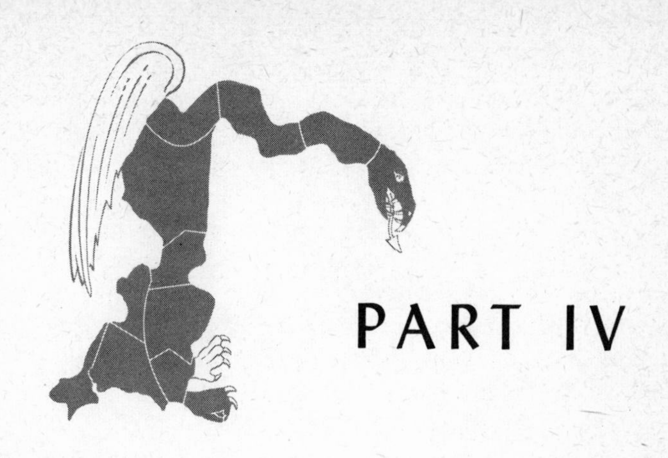

PART IV

Where Do We Go from Here, How to Reapportion?

☆ 11 ☆

GOVERNMENT BY MINORITY

Department of Education and Research, AFL-CIO

This vivid plea for reapportionment is not a model of scholarly detachment, but the cited data on the inequality of districts and gerrymandering are incontrovertible. This expression of the one man-one vote philosophy states the case for apportionment exclusively on the basis of population, and indicates the state constitutional provisions which are obstacles to it. In addition, it furnishes valuable insights into the politics of reapportionment, pointing out that it is neither simply an urban-rural struggle, nor principally a contest between political parties in each state. It is a struggle between competing clusters of interest groups, which perceive that reapportionment distributes political power, and goes a long way toward determining who gets what, when, and how.

When the Declaration of Independence proclaimed all men are created equal and that government must derive its power from the consent of the governed, our founding fathers were expressing their concept of true democracy. Since 1776 each succeeding American generation has faced the task of bringing the nation closer to a fulfillment of these basic American ideals.

For many years after the United States was founded, most of the "governed" were deprived of the right to express their "consent." Only a few Americans were allowed to vote. But over the

Extract from *Government by Minority: the Case for Federal and State Legislative Reapportionment.* Washington: Congress of Industrial Organizations, 1955. Reprinted by permission.

years we have gradually moved forward. Despite poll taxes and other state restrictions which still bar citizens from the ballot box, most of the barriers to voting rights based on property requirements and on factors of race, color, creed, and sex have been whittled away. Today a larger proportion of Americans enjoy the franchise than ever before.

But even the *right* to vote, and its exercise does not in itself insure equal voice in the affairs of government.

Today—more than 175 years after the nation was founded—the votes of millions of citizens are worth only one-half, one-quarter and even one-one hundredth the value of votes of others because of the unfair formulas by which we elect the United States Congress and the legislatures of the forty-eight states. As our population grows and moves continuously toward urban centers, the ballots of millions become less and less equal to the votes of others. Our system of representative government is being sapped at its roots.

How the Minority Rules in the Legislatures

Some years ago the Supreme Court of Kentucky declared:

"Equality is the basis of patriotism. No citizen will or ought to, love the state which oppresses him; and that citizen is arbitrarily oppressed who is denied equality of representation with every other of the Commonwealth."

These words could apply with considerable force to our federal government as well, since millions of American citizens, as we have seen, are being deprived of equal representation in the Congress of the United States. In the legislatures of the states, however, minority rule is becoming so oppressive and has become so widespread, that it has taken on the nature of a national scandal!

Who are the second-class citizens in this underrepresented majority? They are the millions living in our towns and cities, says the United States Conference of Mayors, pointing to the fact that the 59 percent of all Americans who were living in urban centers in 1947 elected only 25 percent of the state legislators.

"59%=25% is bad arithmetic—and bad government. It hurts not just city dwellers, but everybody."

Today, 64 percent of all Americans live in urban centers and each year the proportion continues to rise. Yet the representation of city dwellers in most of the states has hardly increased at all.

Take New Jersey, for example, the most heavily urbanized state in the nation. In the upper house of its state legislature sit eight senators who represent eight counties which contain four-fifths of the population. Outvoting them time after time are thirteen senators from thirteen rural counties who represent only one-fifth of the population of New Jersey.

In Connecticut, the city of Hartford with 177,397 people has two representatives in the lower house; the town of Colebrook with a population of 592 also has two.

In agricultural Iowa, Polk County with 226,010 inhabitants—half of them living in Des Moines—is allowed one senator in the upper house. Mahaska County wiith 24,672 people has one. (The population of Polk County increased 30,000 between 1940 and 1950; Mahaska lost 2,000. Representation? Still one each.)

In California, Los Angeles County with 40 percent of the population, is entitled to only 2½ percent of the state senators.

In Georgia, the 393,000 people who live in Fulton County (Atlanta) had three representatives in the lower house in 1947; Echols County (population 3,000) had one.

Let a legislator from Oregon speak for himself:

> I represent 81,000 people. A few desks away sits a senator from a realm of sagebrush and mountains, and he represents 7,200 people. This is the total population of his district. Any time there is a roll call, regardless of the proposal at issue his vote can cancel mine. The result, of course, is that each resident of this senator's district in the backwoods has eleven times the voice in the state senate of one of my constituents in Portland.

Take a roll call of the forty-eight state legislatures and you will find minority rule almost everywhere. . . .

IN THE BEGINNING, JUST A LITTLE UNDERREPRESENTATION

How, in a great democratic nation, could such a distortion of government "by the people" come about? And why does this injustice continue to this day?

The answer can be found in the resistance of people and institutions to the changes which the growth of America into an urbanized industrial giant has long made overdue.

When the original thirteen states adopted their state constitutions, the 95 percent of the population who lived on isolated farms and in scattered tiny villages were closely tied to their own townships and counties. In that day, it was not surprising that they wanted each township or county to have one representative in the state legislature. In the majority of states today this form of "area" representation, generally by counties, has become established, at least in the makeup of one of the two houses of the state legislature.

Back in 1790 when only 5 percent of the population lived in cities of over 2500, urban areas were so few and their populations were so small, this area form of representation involved only a slight inequity to the city dwellers. . . .

TODAY: A MOCKERY OF DEMOCRACY

But America would not stand still. The age of the frontier and the flintlock, and a nation predominantly made up of farmers, passed away. America's millions began to move to the cities and today a majority of us live there.

But the system by which state legislatures are elected has virtually remained the same.

Look at what this means:

In state after state "area" representation based on townships or counties has made a mockery of representative government.

Although some states have modified their constitutions and now allow large counties two, three, or a few more additional senators (or combine two or three of the smallest counties into one senatorial district), the frustration of inequality of representation continues.

Baltimore, with 47 percent of the population of Maryland, has six out of twenty-nine representatives in its upper house. In New York and Pennsylvania, city representation in the senate is limited to a fixed percentage of the total membership, regardless of population growth.

In Montana, Silver Bow County (Butte) with a population of 48,422 has one senator; Petroleum County with 1,026 has one.

In California the 4,125,146 people who live in Los Angeles County elect one state senator. The 13,568 people who live in the three counties constituting the smallest senatorial district also elect one.

Some state constitutions even freeze unequal representation into the structures of *both* houses of the legislature. Neither is set up to reflect the "respective numbers" in the population as our federal constitution sets forth for the U.S. House of Representatives.

For example, Rhode Island allows a maximum of six senators from any city and a minimum of one representative from any city or town but none to have more than one-fourth of the total.

No Texas county can have more than one senator and not more than seven representatives, except that one additional is allowed for each 100,000 over 700,000.

Wyoming allows at least one seat to each county in both houses, regardless of size.

Delaware froze its division of representatives and senators among the various sections of the state in its constitution of 1897 and hasn't changed it since. . . .

If representation based on townships and counties had some justification 100 years ago—when most of the population was rural and widely dispersed—there can be none today.

Any significance the county may have had in the day of the birchbark canoe or the covered wagon has dwindled in the age of the jet plane and the atom bomb. Besides, our American political system never conferred "sovereign" powers on the counties, such as were enjoyed by the thirteen original sovereign states. There is no parallel in history or in function that can justify a status for the county in the structure of state government comparable to the role of the state in the government of the United States!

But the worst shame of the states is the refusal of the legislatures to reapportion seats according to population changes *even* when the Constitution requires that they do so.

In most of the states representation in at least one house is supposed to reflect population in some degree, as we have seen. *In almost all of the states the constitutions hold the legislators themselves responsible to reapportion legislative seats generally every ten years, after the federal census is conducted. Yet in state after state, as the movement toward the cities has gained momentum, many simply refuse to act.*

Perhaps it was too much to entrust this responsibility to them, since the action inevitably would remove many from their jobs. But even the courts have refused to compel compliance with the clear language of the state constitutions. Both state and federal judges have regularly ruled that they are without power since reapportionment is a "political" and not a "judicial" question.

As a consequence, 22 states have not gotten around to reapportioning even one of the houses of their legislatures in the last ten years or more. The majority of these have not reapportioned for 20, 30, or 40 years, or even longer.

Delaware last established its division of legislative seats in 1897—almost 60 years ago—Alabama in 1901, Minnesota in 1913, Mississippi in 1916, Indiana and Louisiana in 1921. Yet all of these 22 states—except Delaware, Maryland, Montana, and Nebraska, which have no requirements—have specific constitutional or statutory provisions for reapportionment every ten years or less. . . .

Why Progress Stops at the State Line

Is there any wonder why, for the solution of so many vital issues, millions of Americans must look to their federal government instead of the capitols of their states?

While the United States Congress by no means reflects equal representation, its composition is still far more responsive to the needs of America's urban millions than the minority-dominated legislative bodies of most of the forty-eight states.

Even though modern-day problems increasingly require national leadership in this age of industrial interdependence, there is ample scope for constructive action within the states on many issues, if state governments do not default their responsibilities.

Problems like slum clearance, urban traffic congestion, race relations, juvenile delinquency, day nurseries to aid working mothers, health and education, factory safety, workmen's compensation and a score of others plague city people but are often unknown in rural areas. Without adequate funds and state cooperation, cities are powerless to solve these problems unaided. Yet, the rurally dominated legislatures—unfamiliar or unsympathetic to them—too often do little or nothing to help.

Is further intervention by the federal government the only answer? Or can representation in the legislatures of the states be so reconstituted that the needs and views of the urban majority receive attention and get action?

Too often special interest groups—not always originating in the countryside—try to pit farmer against city dweller in an effort to maintain a profitable status quo. . . .

The urban-rural fight over representation is not in reality a conflict between farmers and city citizens. In the states where the issue has been drawn the sharpest, few real "dirt farmers" actually sit in the halls of the legislatures.

The so-called urban-rural rivalry for legislative representation is largely a smokescreen. As Dean McHenry has pointed out with regard to California in the *National Municipal Review*:

> Certain business interests in the state have found it easier to make their influence felt in the legislature through senators from rural areas. Privately owned utilities, banks, insurance companies and other concerns with crucial legislative programs have discovered some "cow-country" legislators more responsive to their demands and less com-

mitted to contrary points of view on key social and economic issues than are urban representatives.

The vigorous opposition of the California Chamber of Commerce (not a dirt farmer organization) to a change in legislative representation more favorable to the cities seems to bear out this view.

Speaking on this issue in 1948, the *Los Angeles Daily News* said:

> The state chamber of commerce's charge that reapportionment would "disenfranchise" the rural counties isn't borne out by analysis. Far from "unbalancing" California's legislature, the proposed measure, if approved next November, would actually restore some semblance of democratic balance to what has been plainly an unbalanced, undemocratic legislative body. . . . Obviously what opponents of reapportionment are trying to do is to manufacture a bit of smog.

Respect for American democracy, both at home and abroad, as well as its ability to fulfill its basic purpose, demands the end of unrepresentative government.

The states are a good place to begin, since it is there that the rotten borough system grows the roots which eventually envelop even our federal congress.

☆ *12* ☆

IN DEFENSE OF COUNTRY VOTES

Noel Perrin

A professor presents here in modern dress the oldest argument for rural overrepresentation—to save "the country" from predatory urban legislators—and for representation of communities rather than by population. Although disavowing the Jeffersonian view of the moral superiority of farmers, this seems to be its actual premise. Much data in support of this anti-equal representation position may be found in the opinions of Justices Frankfurter and Harlan in the Baker *case. One must ask whether farmers are the only people who are occasionally adversely affected by today's public works projects. Rural control of a chamber may have effects other than "saving the countryside."*

Like a very large David standing over a very small Goliath, urban America has been celebrating this year its victory over rural America. In both senses, the victory is a legal one, and the prize, of course, is the control of state legislatures. According to one estimate, about forty of our fifty legislatures will have to reapportion themselves one way or another, if they want to be consonant with the Supreme Court ruling of March, 1962. In all forty cases the effect will be to increase the number of state legislators from cities, and to decrease the number from the country.

Everybody knows why this is happening. Until now, a country

Reprinted by permission from *The Yale Review,* Autumn, 1962, pp. 16–24.

vote has been worth more than a city vote, and often considerably more. In most states, as the then Senator John F. Kennedy of Massachusetts angrily pointed out a few years ago, less than a third of the voters have been able to elect a majority in at least one chamber of the state legislature. Mr. Kennedy cited one extreme case where "13,000 rural voters have as many state senators as four *million* urban dwellers." He could easily have cited others almost as extreme, such as Colebrook, Connecticut, where one vote goes as far to elect a state representative as 205 do in the city of Hartford. . . .

On the face of it, this is a convincing view. Mr. Kennedy, the political scientists, and the cities seem to have every argument on their side. It does indeed look unjust that 13,000 country dwellers should elect as many state senators as four million urbanites do. No one would claim that country people are in any way better, wiser, or more fit to elect state senators than city people are. Equal population, equal vote in the legislature seems the only proper arrangement in a democracy.

But on closer examination, there turn out to be good reasons why legislatures should be weighted in favor of the country. In fact, in many states, so far from rural legislators having had too much influence in recent years, they have probably had too little. The political scientists and urban leaders who are so appalled at the prevailing apportionment seem to have forgotten that the sort of weighting they object to is a traditional and necessary part of representative government. They have turned up little evidence that rural legislators have in fact been frustrating the needs and desires of cities. And they have overlooked considerable evidence that city legislators have ignored and sometimes frustrated the needs and desires of the country even before the recent Supreme Court decision.

First, the matter of tradition and necessity. As most people who took civics in high school know, when our country was founded there was a great debate about what would be the best kind of Congress. Some delegates to the Constitutional Convention wanted to have a congress elected strictly according to population. The majority did not. The majority felt that not only do people need to be represented in a legislature, but also places. Unless we devise a voting chamber where geography rather than population counts, said one of the New Jersey delegates, we leave the small states defenseless. Mr. Oliver Ellsworth of Connecticut agreed. Without a chamber where the states deal as equals, he said, "Four states containing a majority of people will govern nine other states." The result, of course, is our present two houses of Congress.

What the critics of legislatures tend to gloss over is that in every state but one there is also a two-house legislature, and one of these houses is elected by population. There the principle of one man-one vote prevails. (Or at least it will when the new Supreme Court decision is fully enforced. Despite its occasional good uses, I am not arguing in favor of gerrymandering.)

In the other house, in most states, it has been one community, one vote. If this is unjust in a state legislature, it is also unjust in the federal government, where 226,000 people from the community of Alaska elect as many United States senators as almost seventeen million people from the community of New York. It is also unjust in the General Assembly of the United Nations, where 176,000 people from the community of Iceland have as many votes as 438,000,000 people from the community of India. . . .

The second point concerns the way rural state senators vote on city affairs. It is the favorite objection of political scientists that urban affairs are much too important and much too complicated to permit a lot of ignorant farmers in the legislature to have a hand in deciding them. They sometimes conjure up a picture of a league of backwoods legislators, solidly united against cities, and regularly conspiring to block legislation that cities want to have passed. Some such picture may even have been in the minds of some of the Supreme Court justices when they reached their recent decision. The chief trouble with the picture is that it is false. Or, say, 90 percent false.

I know of three studies made in recent years of how rural and city legislators actually do vote. All three seem to show that city members are the ones who are well-organized and who get what they want, while rural members are likely to be disorganized (each one, remember, represents a different community) and to offer no concerted resistance to city legislation. Where cities fail to get what they want, it is generally the result of infighting between city Republicans and city Democrats.

After studying the voting in the Missouri legislature, where St. Louis and Kansas City vie with the mainly rural rest of the state, George D. Young of Missouri concluded: "In the house, the difficulty in passing city legislation does not come from rural members but from members of the city's own delegation. . . . It is almost invariably true that if the city's delegation is united upon a measure, it will be accepted by the entire General Assembly."

Professor David Derge of Indiana University reached much the same conclusion. Professor Derge (who in this matter is a maverick among political scientists) did a statistical analysis of every roll call vote in the Illinois legislature between 1948 and 1958—and votes were called for 14,052 times. He noted, among other things, how Chicago fared at the hands of rural legislators, and decided: "The city's bitterest opponents in the legislature are political enemies from within its own walls, and those camped in the adjoining suburban areas."

Dr. Murray Clark Havens, until recently of the University of Alabama, concluded that even in that predominantly rural state dwellers in cities are far from defenceless: "In the case of rural splits, which were frequent, urban representatives, fairly well united themselves, found it relatively easy to employ the ancient political device of the balance of power." Rural state senators are hardly a threat to city legislation as long as cities have newspapers and television stations and tight political organizations, and the country remains a place where every two townships think differently.

This is not to deny, of course, that there are broad issues on which the country stands solidly opposed to the city, and sometimes gets its way. One such issue in the South at the moment would appear to be integration. Cities seem more disposed to accept it; the country to fight it off. It may be that here really is a case where rural state senators inflict a minority will on the majority of a state's inhabitants. If so, it is a strong point against them.

But even in the case of integration in the South, country legislators may not be the villains that city people usually assume they are. At least one study suggests that they are not. Back in 1950 the departments of psychology and political science at the University of South Carolina joined forces to make a psychological examination of the men then serving in the South Carolina legislature. They wanted to find out what sort of person got elected. It turned out to be a reasonably good sort of person—"far less neurotic than the average male adult, far less introverted, more self-sufficient, and slightly more dominant." This was not very surprising; one doesn't expect to find neurotic introverts doing well in elective politics. But when the study group changed its focus and took a look at the difference between city and country members of the legislature, they got something of a shock. The enlightened city representative and the ignorant backwoodsman were nowhere to be found. Enlightenment and ignorance were about equally distributed. In the words of Professor John B. McConaughey, who wrote up the final report: "The effects of [the] education and urbanity of the electorate upon the political ideas of their representatives are too small to be statistically significant." There is no reason to suppose that this state of affairs is limited to South Carolina.

The third and most important point is that while rural state senators seldom do much harm to cities, urban state assemblymen sometimes do harm the country—and if it weren't for the rural state senators, would perhaps casually wipe out country life altogether. A demonstration could be made using almost any state that contains a large city.

Take the matter of flooding. In Connecticut—a state which political scientists have made a classic example of excessive rural influence—I know of half a dozen country villages which have been wiped out for the sake of one city's water supply. The village I knew best was 170 years old, in good shape physically and financially, and not a bit anxious to die. Furthermore, it stood in the town of Colebrook, and thus each of its citizens had 205 times the representation in the lower house of the Connecticut legislature that citizens of Hartford do. This fact did not save its life. It is true that Hartford needed the water. It is also true that urban Connecticut, so far from being oppressed by the country, is able to extinguish bits of it more or less at will. Actually, the way political scientists describe the situation in Connecticut is somewhat misleading. It is true that in the lower house Hartford and Colebrook have two representatives each. As towns, the two have equal power there. But in the upper house, which is based on population, Hartford has 205 times the power of Colebrook. The Hartford metropolitan area has in the neighboorhood of 1,000 times the power of Colebrook.

Take the same situation in Kansas. Kansas is much more obviously a farm state than Connecticut, and according to the current dogmas of political science the rural inhabitants ought to have things pretty much their own way out there. But they do not. In fact the Kansas Industrial Development Commission advertised a few months ago that Kansas is prepared to flood any reasonable amount of countryside in order to attract new industry. "The biggest change in the Kansas rural landscape in recent years," the Commission reported, "has been the increase in the number and size of water reservoirs. . . . One reservoir now filling will have a permanent water area of 16,000 acres, a shoreline of 112 miles. Large quantities of both surface and ground water are available to meet the needs of most industries." Industry certainly needs water. Countrymen need land. In Kansas, apparently, they lose it to city projects in stretches of twenty-five square miles at a time. . . .

Nor is it just by submersion that urban America is already destroying rural America. It is commonplace to see a country village split in half by a new superhighway rammed through from city to city. I once lived in a small town in New Hampshire which lost its war memorial, its elms, its front yards, and its whole air of serene beauty, simply for a widened feeder road leading to a proposed interstate highway. The highway itself is expected to be along next year.

Or take a more documented case. Dr. Havens, in his pamphlet *City Versus Farm? Urban-Rural Conflict in the Alabama Legislature,* reports the voting in 1955-1956 on the proposal to establish the Alabama Turnpike Authority. His language is difficult, like that of most scholarly reports, but his meaning shines through:

> On three of four roll calls on this subject [building a turnpike], urban legislators demonstrated a decidedly more favorable attitude toward this project than did their mixed and rural colleagues, although proponents were not totally lacking in the latter groups. Some rural opposition was probably due to a possibility that the toll roads constructed would serve primarily to connect the major cities of the state and to carry interstate traffic. The average farmer expects to have little use for such a road system, since many small towns are distant from likely routes. An additional factor was fear in the rural counties through which the turnpike system would pass that condemnation proceedings, under the law of eminent domain, might provide rights of way which would divide individual farms. Since the highways would be of the limited access type, severe economic loss could result in some cases.

This fear in the rural counties did not prevent or even slow up the authorization of the Alabama Turnpike. It did produce an amendment, ensuring fair payment to countrymen whose farms would be split by the turnpike. That seems minimum justice, and it was achieved chiefly through the presence of a large number of rural legislators.

Admittedly, the building of giant highways raises many issues besides rural-urban conflict. The fact remains that highway engineers with city minds plan such roads primarily for city traffic. Their power derives in the end from urban legislators. The welfare of the countryside through which the roads are to run comes a poor second.

City legislators can and do harm the country simply by neglecting it. What happens when high-speed transportation is introduced to a stable city-country relationship can be illustrated by turning to Connecticut again. The chairman of the Committee on Small Towns in the house of the Connecticut General Assembly has put the case well, and he is speaking, it should be understood, of the genuine country districts of central and eastern Connecticut, not of the new exurbia of the west.

With today's transportation, the trend is to work in the city and live in the country, as most people find it a better place to bring up children. The city, with its rail facilities, sewage disposal, and water supplies, continues to attract industry and thereby to increase its tax revenue, while the county districts attract the people and have to pay for the education of the children. In a small town the cost of education may be as high as 80 percent of the total budget, while in the city it may be only 30 percent.

There seems to be no particular reason why a manufacturing company should pay school taxes only to the cities its plants are located in—plants don't go to school—and not to the villages its workers live in. At the time the current school-tax concept came into being, the factories themselves were in the villages, and there was no problem. That system has died, but the tax laws applicable to it remain. They now benefit cities, and urban-dominated legislatures seem content to let it remain so. It is hardly too much to say that the only way a rural village can hope to increase its revenue in 1962 is by deliberately trying to become urban, and that is surrender rather than victory. With some justice, the cities have called a good deal of attention to the facilities, such as hospitals, that they must provide the surrounding countryside. What the countryside provides the city has received less public notice.

What the case for country votes comes to is this. City legislators represent the people of their cities, and the cities themselves. They speak for men and the works of men. Rural legislators represent the small populations of their country districts—and they also speak for their townships and counties, for the land itself. There is quite a difference. For instance, each of the twenty-five state senators from New York City represents about 312,000 people and about 12.6 square miles of land, most of it buried under pavements and buildings. The one state senator who sits for Delaware, Greene, Sullivan, and Ulster Counties represents fewer people—only 240,000—but also more land—4,250 square miles of it. He speaks for something over two hundred towns and villages, scattered over an area a quarter the size of Switzerland. All their diverse interests he must bear in mind. Insofar as anyone does in the state senate, he also speaks for some hundreds of rural valleys, and for a thousand square miles of mountains, filled with wildlife, waterfalls, and forests. All of this he must look out for. It is his job, if it is anyone's, to keep an eye on Kaaterskill Clove, with its triple cascade falling three hundred feet, to make sure it doesn't become simply a power station for some distant but vote-filled city. It is up to him to see that not all the old stone boundary walls in his four counties are turned into road fill for the interstate highway system, and that not all the upland farms become golf courses, or additions to the state park system. (State parks are wonderful for city people, and deserve to exist in large numbers. But a state park is not the country in action, but the country on display. The creation of one means the death of that much more rural life. State park is city zoo writ large.) In short, it is up to him to make sure that the old partnership between man and nature is not dissolved.

Obviously, not every rural legislator sees himself as representing the land as well as the people. People have votes; land does not. But consciously or unconsciously, many rural state senators do speak for mountains as well as men, and should. Their voices deserve to count. If you care whether anything resembling rural life survives; if, like Robert Frost, you say that we belong to our country, as well as that our country belongs to us; if you believe that small nations or small towns have any rights at all against numerically larger neighbors—and one name for this belief is democracy—surely what this country needs is not fewer rural state senators, but more.

☆ 13 ☆

THE FEAR OF URBAN DOMINATION

Howard D. Hamilton, Joseph E. Beardsley, and Carleton C. Coats

Is the preceding impressionistic account of the dangers of urban domination correct or fallacious? Do urban legislators vote as a phalanx to the injury of rural interests? Some light is furnished by the following statistical study of rural-urban influences on voting in the Indiana legislature and by reference to a similar analysis of the Illinois and Missouri legislatures.

The fear that an equitable redistricting would result in domination by city groups with grievous consequences to the state has less basis in Indiana than in many states which have gargantua metropolises. The largest metropolitan area of Indiana has only 15 percent of the state's population and the nine standard metropolitan areas had only 45 percent of the state's population in 1950. This fear appears unfounded for the foregoing reason and also because political party alignments do not coincide with urban-rural areas.

Proponents of the "federal plan" frequently proclaim that a straight population apportionment of the General Assembly would result in domination of the state by five, six, or seven counties. The actual figure would be ten counties which aggregate half of the state's population. This bogey presumes that the representatives and

Extracted from Howard D. Hamilton, Joseph E. Beardsley, and Carleton C. Coats, "Legislative Reapportionment in Indiana: Some Observations and a Suggestion," 35 *Notre Dame Lawyer* 368–402 (May, 1960). Reprinted by permission.

senators from those ten counties would vote solidly to advance their interests—whatever they might be—and to injure the balance of the state. The argument starts from the dubious premise that those ten cities have interests which are distinctive from the interests of the other cities and the rural areas of the state. What issues would produce a solid division of the legislators from the ten most populous counties against those from the other eighty-two counties? Labor issues? Some representatives from those ten counties vote anti-labor (see Tables 1 and 2), and some of the strongest pro-labor legislators are from other counties. Issues involving city government structure and powers? There are large cities outside these ten counties; also these ten counties contain some small cities. Very little "city legislation" concerns the powers and structures of all cities. Such legislation concerns only a class of cities, frequently only one city, although disguised as general legislation. Hence urban representatives do not have a solid, common interest in city legislation. Rural problems and interests? Each of the ten most populous counties—even Marion and Lake—have very substantial rural populations which a legislator would be loathe to antagonize. Issues involving industrial and commercial interests? Although those ten counties necessarily have the greatest concentration of industry and commerce, there are formidable industries and commerce in nearly every corner of Indiana, and no legislator is unmindful of such interests. Furthermore, the lobbyists of industry and commerce make common cause with rural interests in the legislature far more frequently than they oppose them.

The spectre of a dictatorship by a phalanx of legislators from the big cities is exploded by a perusal of recent election statistics, noted above, and by analysis of legislative voting. The writers have made a detailed analysis of the voting behavior of the senators from those ten counties during two recent sessions, 1957 and 1951. Those sessions were selected, because the 1957 session is the most recent one for which the journals have been published and 1951 was a peak year of Democratic Party strength in the senate, the membership consisting of 26 Republicans and 24 Democrats. In 1957, fourteen of the 22 senatorial seats from the districts containing those ten counties were held by Republicans, whereas in 1951 fifteen were held by Democrats.[1] Hence the two sessions present opposite conditions of partisan composition. The votes on third reading roll calls on all controversial bills and resolutions were posted and analyzed, and are summarized in Tables 1 and 2. Controversial roll calls were defined as those in which ten (20 percent) or more senators voted in opposition to the majority vote. This standard was applied in order to eliminate the numerous noncontroversial bills on which there naturally would be no significant difference in the voting of the "metropolitan senators" as compared to the other senators.

Three yardsticks were used to evaluate the voting of the metropolitan senators: the frequency with which a majority of the metropolitan group voted with a majority of the other senators, an index of cohesion of the metropolitan senators, and an index of the likeness of the two groups. The index of cohesion ranges from 0 to 100, with a unanimous vote being 100 and an evenly split vote 0. Thus the overall index of cohesion of 41 for the 1957 session reflects an average voting pattern of 15½ to 6½, and the 37 overall index for the 1951 session reflects an average voting pattern of 15 to 7 on the controversial roll calls.[2] The index of likeness is the complement of the difference between the percentage of affirmative votes of the two groups.[3] Thus the overall index of likeness of 82 in the 1957 session and of 80 in the 1951 session indicates that the percentage of affirmative votes in the respective groups varied by 18 percent in 1957 and 20 percent in 1951.

In Tables 1 and 2 the controversial roll calls are classified according to subject matter, with the corresponding index of cohesion, index of likeness, and number of concurrent majorities. It will be

[1] This included six joint senators with districts including other counties. They were included in the metropolitan group on the assumption that, irrespective of their residences, they would vote with an eye to the residents of the large city in their districts.

[2] Index of Cohesion = 2 (percent of majority vote − 50). This is the frequently used index developed by Stuart A. Rice, *Quantitative Methods in Politics*, 207–210 (1928).

[3] Index of likeness = 100 − (percent of affirmative vote of group A − percent of affirmative vote of group B). The summary data in Tables 1 and 2 are derived from over 3,000 postings and about the same number of arithmetical calculations.

TABLE 1

ANALYSIS OF THE VOTING OF SENATORS FROM THE TEN MOST POPULOUS COUNTIES, INDIANA GENERAL ASSEMBLY, 1957 SESSION

Nature of Bills and Resolutions	Number of Bills	Index of Cohesion	Concurrent Majorities Metropolitan Senators and Other Senators	Index of Likeness of Two Groups
Agriculture and Conservation	6	52	6	86
Alcoholic beverage regulation	3	59	0	53
Business and professional regulation	13	47	10[a]	75
City government	13	33	13	89
County and township government	3	24	2	77
Criminal law	3	35	2	87
Education	7	53	7	81
Labor	8	27	7[a]	85
Motor vehicle and traffic	5	54	5	89
Taxation and revenue	7	39	5[a]	77
Miscellaneous	8	44	7[a]	87
All controversial roll calls	76	41.4	62	81.9

[a] On four other roll calls the senators of one group split their votes evenly.

observed that concurrent majorities prevailed on 62 of the 76 controversial roll calls in 1957 and on 41 of the 63 in 1951. On five other bills a group split its votes evenly. Such a record hardly reflects a sharp clash between the metropolitan senators and their peers. Similarly, the overall index of likeness of 82 in 1957 and 80 in 1951 demonstrates a strong similarity in the voting behavior of the two groups.

In the 1957 session only one class of bills, those pertaining to alcoholic beverage regulation, aligned a majority of the metropolitan senators against a majority of the nonmetropolitan solons. In the 1951 session there were no concurrent majorities on the three controversial bills pertaining to agriculture and conservation, but, interestingly, in 1957 concurrent majorities occurred on all six bills in that category. Hence alcoholic beverage regulation was the only category which consistently produced a metropolitan *v.* nonmetropolitan pattern.

Other categories in which one might anticipate such an alignment showed scant disagreement between the two groups. Thus on the ten labor bills in both sessions concurrent majorities prevailed nine times and one group split evenly on the other one. On the

TABLE 2

ANALYSIS OF VOTING OF SENATORS FROM THE TEN MOST POPULOUS COUNTIES, INDIANA GENERAL ASSEMBLY, 1951 SESSION

Nature of Bills and Resolutions	Number of Bills	Index of Cohesion	Concurrent Majorities Metropolitan Senators and Other Senators	Index of Likeness of Two Groups
Agriculture and Conservation	3	32	0	75
Business regulation	6	47	5	83
City government	5	33	4	84
Civil law and procedure	7	47	5[a]	81
County and township government	10	47	6	74
Criminal law	4	17	2	86
Education	2	51	1	81
Labor	2	43	2	76
Motor vehicles and traffic	5	30	4	89
Taxation and revenue	9	32	4	84
Miscellaneous	10	27	8	73
All controversial roll calls	63	36.9	41	80.1

[a] Senators of one group split vote evenly on another bill.

eighteen city government bills, seventeen concurrent majorities occurred and one group split on the other one. On the nineteen bills relating to business and professional regulation, concurrent majorities occurred on fifteen bills and one group split on another. For the other categories, concurrent majorities also were the pattern, as one might expect. The index of likeness was 73 or above on all categories except alcoholic beverage regulation.

The indices of cohesion among the metropolitan group were almost uniformly low in both sessions. Even on the alcoholic beverage bills, which elicited the most cohesion, the group split 17 to 5. On labor bills the average vote was 14 to 9 in 1957 and 15½ to 7½ in 1951. On city government bills the group split on the average of 15 to 8 in both sessions, and voted with corresponding majorities of the other group on both labor and city government bills. The metropolitan group never voted solidly on anything controversial in either session.

The low indices of cohesion among the metropolitan senators, an overall of 41 in 1957 and 37 in 1951, furnish a sharp contrast to the indices of cohesion among senators of the respective political parties. On the same controversial roll calls in 1951, the Republican members displayed an index of cohesion of 87.1 and the Democrats 89.3.

The foregoing data conclusively show that political party affiliation in the Indiana General Assembly is a stronger influence than whether the solon hails from a metropolitan or a "rural" district. Rural-urban, or metropolitan *v.* nonmetropolitan, conflict is *not* a strong factor in the General Assembly. Metropolitan senators do not vote as a phalanx, they generally divide their votes in about the same manner as their colleagues, and the bogey of a metropolitan dictatorship in the legislature in the event of a fair reapportionment is a myth.

These results concur with a similar study of votes in the Illinois and Missouri legislatures, which reported:

> [G]enuine metropolitan against nonmetropolitan conflict in the Illinois and Missouri General Assemblies is rare. . . . Further, collision

of urban-rural interests, as forwarded by legislators from those two areas, is seldom found, while conflict of interests within the urban areas frequently appears in the legislature.[4]

The reasons for the low cohesion among the metropolitan senators are hardly obscure: the obvious one of party affiliation, which is a stronger force in the Indiana General Assembly than in some legislatures; the irrelevance of population density to the bulk of legislation, and the complexity of the political and social structure of the metropolitan community which proliferates competing interests.

The fear of urban dictatorship is the product of widespread misunderstanding, a misunderstanding which is being sedulously cultivated by the proponents of the "federal plan." Professor Gordon Baker has correctly sized up this matter.

> While a granting of urban representation proportionate to population would not result in a single, cohesive urban "majority," it could effectuate a considerable shift in the pattern of political power. Some urban interests that formerly had little influence would probably gain more, while others (notably those that enjoy an advantage from an alliance with rural forces) would lose. It is this potential shift in the power equilibrium that arouses the greatest resistance from the elements benefiting from the status quo. That resistance is prompted by a fear not of *an* urban interest, but of *certain* urban interests.[5]

[4] Derge, David, "Metropolitan and Outstate Alignments in the Illinois and Missouri Legislative Delegations," 52 *Am. Pol. Sci. Rev.* 1052 (1958).

[5] Baker, Gordon E., *Rural Versus Urban Political Power,* Random House, 1955.

☆ 14 ☆

CURRENT BASES OF REPRESENTATION AND THE "FEDERAL PLAN"

David H. Everson and Howard D. Hamilton

The yokels hang on because old apportionments give them unfair advantages. The vote of a malarious peasant on the lower Eastern Shore counts as much as the votes of twelve Baltimoreans. But that can't last. It is not only unjust and undemocratic; it is absurd.

H. L. MENCKEN

There are ninety-nine state legislative chambers and almost as many apportionment formulae. Consequently any effort to summarize, either in a table as below, or narratively, is an over simplification and likely to be misleading. Thus a recent scholarly opus informs us that "Only nine states apportion their legislatures on the basis of population." And elsewhere one learns that "Population is the standard basis for apportionment; it is used in all states except Delaware's permanent districts, which originally were drawn according to population." Both statements are correct, as far as they go, and both are misleading. The first overlooks the fact that population is basically the standard in many other states and that such alternatives as Arizona's "votes cast for governor," Indiana's "males over twenty," Massachusetts' "legal voters," and Tennessee's "qualified voters" are not profoundly different from popula-

TABLE 1

BASES OF POPULATION APPORTIONMENT, 1964

Unqualified	Qualified: One Chamber	Qualified: Two Chambers	House only; Senate: Fixed Districts	Fixed Districts Both Chambers
Indiana	Alaska	Alabama	Arizona[q]	Delaware
Kentucky	California	Connecticut	Arkansas[q]	
Massachusetts	Kansas	Florida	Colorado	
Minnesota	Michigan	Georgia	Hawaii	
Oregon	Missouri	Iowa	Idaho*[q]	
South Dakota	Nebraska[u]	Louisiana	Illinois	
Tennessee	New Hampshire[t]	Maine	Maryland*[q]	
Virginia	North Carolina	New York	Mississippi[q]	
Washington	Ohio	Pennsylvania	Montana*	
West Virginia	Oklahoma	Rhode Island	Nevada*[q]	
Wisconsin	Utah	Texas	New Jersey*[q]	
		Vermont	New Mexico*	
		Wyoming	North Dakota[q]	
			South Carolina*[q]	

[q] Qualified population for House. [u] Unicameral legislature.
[t] Senate apportioned according to direct taxes. * Each county has one senator.
SOURCE: *Book of the States*, 1961–1962, adjusted for later developments.

tion as bases of representation. Equally insignificant is the exclusion of aliens from the base in a few states. The second quotation glosses over the fact that population is qualified in some manner in apportioning half of the chambers of the country, some of the qualifications being of negligible effect and others virtually wiping out the population standard.

Nevertheless, unless one wishes a table of ninety-nine categories or footnotes, some generalization is imperative. The soundest and most fundamental generalization is that population continues to be the primary and preeminent principle for structuring legislatures, notwithstanding strenuous efforts by potent pressure groups to scuttle it in many states. Eleven state constitutions prescribe it for both chambers without significant qualifications. It is to be used with a variety of qualifications for one or both chambers of thirty-eight other states. Only Delaware has entirely ignored it, by freezing all its districts into its constitution in 1897, but post-*Baker* the Delaware legislature redistricted with some recognition of population. The most quaint departure from the population principle is New Hampshire's senate, which is apportioned among the towns (New England towns) according to "direct taxes paid," but that basis seems to produce results which approximate population.

Of the ninety-nine chambers, thirty-seven are based on population unqualified (appreciably), forty-six on population qualified, and fifteen are composed of fixed districts prescribed in constitutions. The fixed districts of seven states are counties, the constitution assigning one senator for each county. The other fixed districts came about by incorporating an existing districting pattern of the senate (both chambers in Delaware) into the constitution, e.g., Arkansas in 1956, North Dakota in 1960, and Colorado in 1962.[1] Such action is a deliberate abandonment of the population principle and, as time goes by, discrepancies in representation are bound to grow. In an era of high population mobility, freezing any districting pattern into the constitution is a dubious policy.

The state constitutional provisions which qualify the population principle and their effects are lucidly summarized by Professor Clyde F. Snider:

> A type of constitutional provision which fosters urban underrepresentation is that requiring equal representation of counties or towns, regardless of population. . . . [Another] type limits urban representation indirectly by providing that each county or town shall have at least one member. Since a provision of this type is commonly accompanied by a limitation upon the total membership of the house concerned, its usual effect is to allot so many of the members to rural areas that too few remain to afford adequate representation to the more populous counties. . . . [A third] type of restrictive constitutional provision sets an upper limit upon the number of legislative members which any county or town may have.[2]

A fourth type has appeared very recently, an apportionment formula which combines the factors of population and area for the composition of one chamber.

[1] Hawaii and Alaska began statehood by writing senate districts into the constitution.

[2] *American State and Local Government* (New York: 1950), pp. 170–171.

Each county or (in New England) town is accorded at least one seat in twenty-eight chambers of twenty-four states (in addition to the seven state senates of one seat per county). Thus we come to the second major basis of apportionment: local subdivisions or communities. Whether counties are communities today is debatable, but they were in the infancy of each state. When the nation was agrarian, representation for each county or town did not greatly diverge from the population principle, but today it usually produces glaring discrepancies in representation.

TABLE 2

LOCAL SUBDIVISION: AS A BASIS OF APPORTIONMENT, 1964

Counties or Towns Guaranteed One Seat				One Senator per County
House		Senate	Both	
Alabama	Missouri	Maine	Connecticut	Idaho
Arkansas	Montana		Rhode Island	Maryland
Connecticut	New Jersey		Vermont	Montana
Florida	New York		Wyoming	Nevada
Georgia	North Carolina			New Jersey
Idaho	North Dakota			New Mexico
Iowa	Ohio			South Carolina
Kansas	Pennsylvania			
Louisiana	South Carolina			
Mississippi				

The effect of the combination of the two bases, population and subdivisions, depends on the distribution or dispersion of the population of a state and the ratio of the number of seats in a chamber to the number of counties or towns. Thus the population principle becomes the subordinate factor in the Kansas house of representatives of 125 members and 105 counties, leaving only 20 seats to be apportioned according to population. Population is almost negligible in the Iowa house of representatives with 108 seats and 99 counties. On the other hand, districting might approximate population in the Alabama house, 106 seats and 67 counties, or the New York house, 150 seats and 74 counties.

The other prevalent qualification of population is a constitutional limit on the number of seats for any county, city, or town. Thus no county may have more than one-sixth of the senators in Pennsylvania nor more than one-third the senators in New York—and two adjacent counties no more than one-half. A Rhode Island city may have only one-fifth of the representatives. Seven representatives are the maximum for a Maine town and an Oklahoma county. Far more severe are the ceilings in California and Iowa where no county may have more than one senator. That ceiling in California is combined with a provision that a senatorial district shall have no more than three counties; thereby Los Angeles' six million people have the same representation as a mountain district of 14,294 people!

Tables 1 and 2, and the preceding narrative are based on the texts of state constitutions as of March 1, 1964, several of which were being amended at that time. Also the provisions of some of the states which severely qualify the population principle, or disregard it entirely by fixed districts, have been held by state and federal courts to violate the Fourteenth Amendment in the light of *Baker* v. *Carr*. Those decisions, except a Michigan case which became moot, are before the Supreme Court for review and their outcome may overturn the constitutional provisions of many states.

Developments After *Baker* v. *Carr*

What has happened in the two years since the *Baker* decision? One discernible trend has been a widespread effort to write some version of the so-called "federal plan" into state constitutions. Such plans were adopted in Colorado, Nebraska, Michigan, and North Dakota; rejected by the Kansas and Mississippi legislatures and the electorates of Iowa, Oregon, North Carolina and West Virginia; held invalid by federal courts in Alabama and Virginia; and one is pending further action in Indiana.

Seven states have redistricted one or both chambers under the rules of their constitutions.[3] Kansas did it twice, after the first effort was held defective by the state courts. The results have varied,

[3] Florida, Indiana, Kansas, Kentucky, Louisiana, North Carolina, and Vermont.

ranging from Kentucky where the apportionment is said to be "second to Oregon in compliance with pure population equality,"[4] to other states where the changes were only minimal.

A comedy of errors occurred in Indiana where a reapportionment bill in 1963 was vetoed by the governor, who said that although the bill was an improvement over the previous apportionment (1921), it contained features "neither constitutional nor fair."[5] A year later the state courts ruled that the veto was tardy and that the revised districts were applicable to the primary elections a few weeks hence. To compound the confusion, the statute inadvertently provided for more senators than the state constitution authorizes.

Two states have been reapportioned by federal courts, the most far-reaching judicial action to date in the wake of *Baker* v. *Carr*. (The prospect of reapportionment by the courts in the event of legislative default was a potent stimulus to all the legislatures in their 1963 sessions.) In Oklahoma, the court ruled the apportionment invalid and decreed that the legislature should reapportion at its 1963 session on the "principle of substantial equality," which was the general standard of the state constitution.[6] The court explicitly held that the state constitutional limit of seven representatives to a county violated the Fourteenth Amendment and should be disregarded. The legislature did redistrict, but failed to observe the court's standard of population equality. Thereafter the court decreed an apportionment of both chambers, effective until the 1970 census.[7] In Alabama, the court decreed an apportionment (superseding an apportionment of 1901) for the 1963 election only, the pattern consisting of elements of two plans which had been discussed in the legislature. The court opined that its temporary and "moderate" action would break the "stranglehold" and enable the legislature to enact a fair apportionment.[8]

In addition to the four "federal plan" adoptions, nine states have modified their systems of representation. In five states reapportion-

[4] *National Civic Review*, April, 1963, p. 207. Hereafter cited as *NCR*.
[5] *Indiana Senate Journal*, Spring, Summer, 1963, p. 12.
[6] *Moss* v. *Burkhart*, 207 F. Supp. 878 (1962).
[7] *NCR*, September, 1963, p. 446.
[8] *Sims* v. *Frink*, 208 F. Supp. 431 (1962).

ment was coupled with expansion of one or both chambers to give some relief to underrepresented areas.[9] Georgia revised its senate districts after a court held the former apportionment unconstitutional,[10] and Hawaii made slight boundary adjustments.[11] Idaho, Utah, and Wyoming adopted similar patterns of a representative for a specified population and additional representatives for specified increments. Thus Idaho allotted one for the first 5,000 inhabitants of a county and an additional one for each 10,000 inhabitants.[12]

The most novel and spectacular innovation is New Mexico's weighted voting system adopted in 1963, the first experiment with that oft-discussed idea. The 77 members of the revised house would cast a total of 700 votes, scaled from 10 votes for each legislator from the twenty largest (populous) counties to 1 for the representatives of the twelve smallest counties.[13] This is an imaginative scheme for killing two birds: providing population equality and, at the same time, a representative for each county. It might be said that the system does not fully achieve equality, because a populous county has only two or three representatives to shepherd its local bills and sit on committees. The power or influence of a legislator is not exclusively in voting on roll calls. Unfortunately, a local court already has pronounced the scheme invalid as not being authorized by the state constitution.[14]

Proposed apportionments have been defeated in several states, e.g., the federal plans rejected by the electorates of Iowa, Oregon, West Virginia, and North Carolina, and held invalid by courts in Virginia and Alabama. Electorates also rejected a proposal to guarantee a representative to each county in West Virginia,[15] an initiated proposal to reapportion the Washington legislature on the basis of population equality,[16] and a proposal to grant ten more

[9] Delaware, Florida, Idaho, Mississippi, and Utah.

[10] *Toombs* v. *Forteson,* 205 F. Supp. 248 (1962).

[11] *NCR,* December, 1962, p. 623.

[12] *State Government News,* April, 1963, p. 3. Hereafter cited as *SGN.*

[13] *NCR,* January, 1964, p. 35. The eighteen members from Bernadillo County (Albuquerque) would cast 180 votes.

[14] *SGN,* February, 1964, p. 3.

[15] *NCR,* December, 1962, p. 623.

[16] *Ibid.*

senators to the grossly underrepresented metropolises of California.[17] An apportionment bill in Rhode Island, enacted after a state court ruled invalid the constitutional guarantee of at least one seat for every town, was vetoed.[18] In Tennessee, an apportionment, ordered by the federal court in the still continuing case of *Baker* v. *Carr,* was enacted in 1963 and promptly ruled invalid for being "irrational" and discriminating against the metropolitan areas.[19]

The recalcitrance of the Tennessee, Oklahoma, Maryland, and some other legislatures reminds one of H.L. Mencken's comment four decades ago. But, as he predicted, "that can't last," and the old order changeth apace. Every week or so, it seems, a court holds an apportionment invalid and mandates another, a governor convenes the legislature in special session, or the electorate of some state votes on an apportionment amendment. Following the electoral defeat of the "federal plan" in Iowa, December, 1963, the court which had held the Iowa apportionment invalid ordered the legislature to provide an interim reapportionment by June for the 1964 elections—or presumably the court would.[20]

Confusion in Illinois

The veto of an apportionment bill enacted in the closing gasp of the 1963 Illinois legislature will apparently result in a spectacular debacle without parallel in American politics: an at-large election in 1964 of the 177 members of the Illinois house, on the longest ballot in American history. This ballot may have over 400 names!

The spectre which Justice Frankfurter conjured up in the *Colegrove* case as one of the reasons why courts should never cast eyes on an apportionment law has come to life, and in the very state of Illinois, but not because his colleagues subsequently disregarded his admonition and temerariously entered the "political thicket."

[17] *Ibid.*
[18] *NCR*, September, 1963, p. 450.
[19] *SGN*, November, 1963, p. 5.
[20] *Ibid.*, February, 1964, p. 3.

The Illinois snafu was not caused by judicial intervention; it is not one of the progeny of *Baker* v. *Carr*. It is an unforeseen result of the Illinois constitutional amendment of 1954, which broke a forty-year apportionment deadlock and established an Illinois version of a "federal plan."

The 1954 apportionment article, which froze the new senate districts, requires redistricting of the house on a population basis in 1963 and every decade. To coerce the legislature, which procrastinated from 1901 to 1954, the article stipulates that in the exigency of default by the legislators, apportionment shall devolve to an ad hoc commission, and if it defaults, the ensuing election shall be at-large. It was assumed that the fear of being districted by an alien body, reinforced by the even greater fear of an at-large election, would be adequate incentive for the legislature, and in consequence, neither of the alternatives would ever materialize.

The legislature strove mightily to avert catastrophe, but the Democrats and Republicans quarreled to the bitter end on the distribution of the house districts between the three regions demarcated by the 1954 article: Chicago (Democratic), Cook County suburbs (Republican), and the 101 counties Downstate (Republican). (Under the cumulative voting system of minority representation, nearly all the three-member districts divide in elections 2 to 1 on the basis of party, producing a house membership which corresponds closely with the statewide popular vote.) The Democratic delegation insisted that because the "federal plan" permanently discriminates against Chicago, making the senate constitutionally Republican, that loss should be offset by the house districting. In the wee hours, the Republican majority forced through its districting bill and the Democratic governor vetoed it. The hope of an eleventh hour bipartisan "deal" failed to materialize.

Thereupon the governor followed the procedures of the apportionment article by appointing a bipartisan reapportionment commission of five members from lists submitted by the political parties. Thus the commission, by its structure, perpetuated the same partisan views as the preceding legislature, and it remained stalemated until its mandate expired.

In early 1964, a special session of the legislature enacted temporary laws providing for state nominating conventions in place of the regular primaries, prescribing a separate ballot for the election of members of the house of representatives, and specifying that each party might nominate a maximum of 118 candidates to run from the state at large. No provision was made for culmulative voting, although cumulative voting is specified in the Illinois constitution. A candidate can still be nominated from the state at large, but he must secure at least 200 signatures to his nominating petition from each county—a formidable obstacle for an independent candidate. The Illinois Supreme Court upheld these laws, averring that the cumulative voting provision of the constitution applies only to election of house members by districts, not from the state at large. In 1964, therefore, house members of the Illinois legislature will be elected from the state at large, and it is expected that most of the incumbent representatives will be nominated by convention and re-elected to office.

There is more than one moral in the saga of the Illinois debacle: (1) People of communities, parties, and interest groups which are permanently underrepresented by some "federal plan" are likely to remain dissatisfied even though the formula is embalmed in the state constitution, and occasionally they can find a means of expressing their feelings. (2) Repeated defaults by a legislature of its reapportionment obligation are not solely because of self-interest or procrastination, but are also due to partisan legislatures reaching stalemates on how to reapportion. (3) The vested interests of incumbent legislators, both personal and partisan, make them unsuitable for reapportioning, for they must judge their own situations. (4) Therefore, the function probably should be transferred entirely to a reapportionment commission, as was done recently by Alaska and Michigan. (5) The Illinois ad hoc commission is structurally defective.

Had the commission been an ex officio body composed of the governor and two or three others, it might have lacked objectivity but it could have done the job. (That is the arrangement of such alternative agencies in a dozen states.) The Illinois commission lacked any objectivity and thus had no capacity to act at all. To have the members appointed by the political parties is the worst possible arrangement. Calhoun's concurrent majorities theory is useful for routine legislation, indeed it is the standard modus operandi of legislatures, but structuring the commission on that principle was a disastrous error. A better design for a reapportionment commission, whether with exclusive or only alternative jurisdiction, would be to use unpartisan members, as in Alaska and the United Kingdom.[21]

Federal Plans

Several of the lawsuits since *Baker* v. *Carr* are challenges of various apportionment formulae which are styled "federal plans." In early 1964 appeals from Colorado, Maryland, and Virginia were on the Supreme Court's docket, and more will follow. To date, the state and federal court decisions have differed; such systems have been held invalid by the Michigan Supreme Court and federal courts in Alabama and Virginia, and sustained by the Maryland supreme court and federal courts in Colorado and Illinois.[22] The decisions are not necessarily irreconcilable, because some federal plans are less discriminatory than others, as a recent brief for the new Michigan plan goes to great pains to show.[23]

[21] House of Commons constituencies are revised by "boundary commissions" appointed by Mr. Speaker, the paragon of nonpartisanship. In Alaska a commission of private citizens, appointed by the governor, prepares the districting pattern, which the governor may modify if he states his reasons in the promulgation.

[22] Respectively, *Scholle* v. *Hare,* 367 Mich. 176 (1962); *Sims* v. *Frink,* 208 F. Supp. 431 (1962); *Mann* v. *Davis,* 213 F. Supp. 577 (1962); *Md. Comm. for Fair Rep.* v. *Tawes,* 229 Md. 406 (1962); *Lisco* v. *Love,* 219 F. Supp. 922 (1963); *Germano* v. *Kerner,* 220 F. Supp. 230 (1963). The Michigan case, holding the 1952 plan invalid, was mooted by adoption of a new constitution in 1963. The Virginia case opinion was speculatory, because population is the Virginia rule.

[23] Karl A. Lamb *et al., Apportionment and Representative Institutions, the Michigan Experience* (Washington, 1963).

The expression apparently was coined as a description and rationale of the 1926 amendment in California which established the aforementioned senate apportionment formula. It spread around the country in the 1950's as apportionment controversies brewed in many states. The term is ambiguous. The essence of some apportionments to which the tag has been attached is permanent senate districts frozen in constitutions. Often the label is applied to those senates in which each county has one—and only one—seat; sometimes even more broadly to any legislature where every county or town is guaranteed a minimum of one seat. Frequently it is defined as "one house based on population and the other on area." That is palpably erroneous, for there is no legislative chamber in the United States "based on area," and the Illinois senate formula of 1954 was the first to have area as one factor. Most of the apportionments which have been said to be by area actually have arrangements for representation of local subdivisions, as listed in Table 2.

The arrangement in some New England states of at least one representative for every town (it must be an inhabited town in New Hampshire), and in the several states which guarantee a seat to every county, antedates the "federal plan" phrase by a few centuries, and surely did not originate by analogy to Congress. The intent was simply to afford representation to every community, and until the twentieth century the districting usually approximated population and was satisfactory. Indubitably, such districts were not originally designed to underrepresent metropolitan areas. Hence it would seem that there are only nine states, classified in Table 3, which have authentic "federal plans," deliberately designed to underrepresent metropolitan or urban areas.

Michigan has had two systems and Illinois appears in the table three times, because its unique system has three elements. The Illinois article assigns permanently 18 senate seats to Chicago, 6 to the balance of Cook County, and 34 Downstate. "Area shall be the prime consideration" in drawing senate districts; house districts continue to be of equal population.[24] The article does

[24] The legislature actually drew the senate districts with more attention to incumbents and politics than the "prime consideration" of area.

not say that the senate districts shall be permanent, but the Illinois courts so ruled during the 1964 controversy. The allocation slightly overrepresents surburban Cook County (Republican) and gives Downstate (Republican) four extra seats at the expense of Chicago (Democratic). This is less discriminatory than the apportionments of many states, and fairer by far than the apportionment formulae of such urban states as California, Connecticut, Maryland, New Jersey, or Rhode Island.

TABLE 3

FEDERAL PLANS

I. Districts delineated or otherwise frozen in a state constitution:

Alaska (1956)	Illinois (1954)
Arkansas (1956)	Michigan (1952)
Colorado (1962)	North Dakota (1960)
Hawaii (1959)	

II. Area as one factor in apportionment of senate:

Illinois (1954)	Nebraska (1963)
Michigan (1963)	

III. Other arrangements:

California (1926) senate maxima: 1 senator to a county, 3 counties to a district

Illinois (1954): senate seats distributed to three regions

The full potential of "federal plans" is illustrated by one passed by the Indiana house (before *Baker* v. *Carr*) which proposed to reduce the house membership to 92, assigning each seat to one county. Thus the ten urban counties would have had their representation reduced from 51 percent to which they are proportionally entitled (they actually have only 38 percent) to 11 percent. The greatest disparity in a federal plan chamber is the 428 to 1 ratio of the largest and smallest California senate districts. That record is contested by some of the Atlantic states which have retained their traditional, perhaps colonial, patterns of equal representation for the towns or counties: the New Jersey senate districts have a maximum ratio of 19 to 1, the Rhode Island senate of 95 to 1, and the Connecticut house of 162 to 1.

The 1926 California senate revision probably was the first "federal plan," a system which deliberately abandoned the population principle, in order to undercut the political influence of large and growing cities and to establish a rural (i.e., nonmetropolitan) "stranglehold" on the legislature.

The next intentional federal plan was the Michigan constitutional amendment of 1952, pushed by an alliance of the farm bureau, the chambers of commerce, and local officialdom, and warmly approved by the Republican party. It froze the existing senate districts, an antiquated apportionment which grossly under-represented the Detroit metropolitan area.

Although Michigan abandoned the plan simultaneously with its invalidation by the state court, Arkansas, Colorado and North Dakota have imitated it. That species of federal plan is the most vulnerable one in the light of *Baker* v. *Carr*. Freezing an antiquated districting can hardly be said not to produce an apportionment that is "irrational" and "invidiously discriminatory," two tests which trial courts have seized on from the *Baker* opinions. The Colorado law has some chance of survival, because the freezing amendment simultaneously reapportioned a little, giving four additional seats to the metropolitan areas.

The California senate formula and the ancient patterns of one seat per county or a seat for every town or county, particularly in those states which consequently have fantastic disparities in representation, certainly are vulnerable as "irrational" (now) and "invidious discrimination."

The Colorado case poses an intriguing question which may consume a quantity of judicial ink. What about the referendum factor and the availability in a state of the popular initiative (noted by Justice Clark in *Baker*)? Should an apportionment with "invidious discrimination" be ruled unconstitutional if it is ratified by the people? A familiar reply is that federal constitutional rights cannot be nullified by any state internal arrangements or practices. But is an apportionment really "irrational" or "invidious" if endorsed by a majority of the electorate? And, more fundamentally, should a state be compelled by the federal judiciary to have fair representation if the majority does not want it? In Rousseau's words, should the people be "forced to be free?" A rebuttal to the latter argument would be that it is the Fourteenth Amendment, not the judiciary, which compels the people to be free.

Maryland is one of the states whose senate for a century has consisted of a senator for each county (plus four for Baltimore City). The house apportionment was written into the constitution in 1867, modified slightly thereafter, and the districts were frozen in 1950. Thus by 1962, Maryland had the distinction of an ossified legislature, probably the most unrepresentative in the country. Suburbanites failed repeatedly to secure redress in the legislature, so in 1960 they went to court. The Maryland courts first ducked behind the "political question" blind, but the *Baker* case eliminated that refuge. Then the state courts ruled the frozen house districts violative of the Fourteenth Amendment, and the legislature hastily redistricted, granting nineteen additional seats to suburban counties and Baltimore. The Committee for Fair Representation also challenged the senate apportionment, but the Maryland court regarded the revised situation as a federal plan and constitutional.[25] The Committee petitioned the Supreme Court for review.

The latest and most curious wrinkle is the 80–20 formula, a senate apportioned 80 percent by population and 20 percent by area, which became effective almost simultaneously in Michigan and Nebraska in 1963. That arbitrary formula apparently was invented in a resolution of the Nebraska unicameral legislature to alter its own apportionment base to allow a 20 percent to 30 percent consideration of area. The subsequent apportionment weights the two factors 80–20.[26]

The identical formula was adopted in 1962 by a Michigan con-

[25] *Comm. for Fair Repr.* v. *Tawes,* 229 Md. 406 (1962).

[26] *NCR,* June, 1963, p. 326. As Adam Smith might say, "the invisible hand of providence" was working simultaneously in Nebraska and Michigan.

stitutional convention, in high excitement, a few hours after the Michigan court rendered the preceding federal plan invalid. The convention leaders read *Baker* as indicating that the 80–20 formula would survive the inevitable legal assault, and promptly some delegates and staff produced a hefty treatise to be used in the courts to defend it. The constitution, which was ratified in a warm and close referendum (over the apportionment issue) reads:

> In districting the state for the purpose of electing senators, . . . each county shall be assigned apportionment factors equal to the sum of its percentage of the state's population as shown by the last regular federal decennial census computed to the nearest one-one hundredth of 1 percent multiplied by 4 and by its percentage of the state's land area computed to the nearest one-one hundredth of 1 percent.

Senate seats are distributed according to the factor points of a county or combination of counties, but within a county districts are to have equal population. The formula operates to make nineteen acres of land equal to one person (by 1980, thirteen acres) and some sparsely settled parts of the Upper Peninsula will be entitled to seats even if entirely uninhabited. An amendment at the convention inserted "land," thereby depriving lakes of representation. One may wonder how the stumps in the Michigan cutover country will vote now that they have the singular dignity of representation in the legislature.

The defenders of the status quo in the 1963 Indiana General Assembly copied the Michigan plan, but instead of assigning one-fifth of the senate to area, the proposed constitutional amendment assigns "one-fifth of a senator" to each of the 92 counties, 37 percent of the senate membership.

Any species of federal plan will have numerous and profound effects—else who would want it? One highly visible effect is the impact on political parties, as illustrated by Table 4. It will be observed that in the eight elections the Democratic party garnered the largest popular vote five times, but never won the "federal" chamber. The Democrats cannot possibly win the senate in either Illinois or Michigan. In Al Smith's immortal words, "the legislature is constitutionally Republican." The degree to which a federal plan stacks the cards in favor of party depends on the correlation of the party vote with the overrepresented and underrepresented regions of a state. Where party strength is rather uniformly distributed over a state, as in Indiana, a federal plan will have less impact on elections.

In such states a Democratic governor invariably faces a hostile majority in the "federal" chamber, with the attendant friction and stalemate. In the years when the Republican party loses other offices it retains control of the senate. In the years that the Republican party *and* its allied interest groups win the election, they are in a position to enact legislation they desire; in the years that the

TABLE 4
IMPACT OF "FEDERAL PLAN" ON POLITICAL PARTY STRENGTH IN LEGISLATURES

	Illinois		Michigan	
	Republicans	Democrats	Republicans	Democrats
Election of 1956				
Popular vote[a]	2,172	2,135	1,376	1,667
House seats	94	83	61	49
Senate seats	38	18	23	11
Election of 1958				
Popular votes[a]	1,549	1,689	1,075	1,214
House seats	86	91	55	55
Senate seats	34	24	22	12
Election of 1960				
Popular vote[a]	2,070	2,595	1,602	1,643
House seats	89	88	56	54
Senate seats	31	27	22	12
Election of 1962				
Popular vote[a]	1,961	1,748	1.421	1,341
House seats	90	87	58	52
Senate seats	35	23	23	11

[a] Popular vote is in thousands for the top statewide election: governor or senator.

Republicans and their allies lose the election, they can block any legislation they dislike. It is difficult to see how such a system can be called just or representative government.

More important than these effects is the impact on the various interest groups. The federal chamber tends to favor rural, business, native white, and conservative groups, and oppose urban or metropolitan, labor, ethnic minority, and liberal groups. The former gain advantages for affirmative legislation and always are in a position to veto what they oppose. This is what "TR" called "real politics." Any federal plan profoundly affects who gets what, when and how.

Frequently it is said that rural (actually small city) people should dominate one chamber in order to protect the countryside against predatory urban legislators. That contention overlooks two facts of life. (1) Interests other than farmers are also aided by a chamber designed to underrepresent metropolitan people. The arrangement affects the whole gamut of legislation: taxes, education, welfare, etc. (2) Any districting which enables rural areas to have a veto over issues of peculiar concern to them, also gives them—and their particular city allies—a veto over everything else.

The principal arguments for federal plans were succinctly stated by a Maryland county judge:

> Such an arrangement protects the minorities. It prevents hasty, although popular, legislation at the time. It is based upon history and reason and helps to protect the republican form of government. . . . It preserves the checks and balances of the state government which has worked so well under the federal. Moreover, there would be little advantage in having a bicameral legislature if the composition and the qualifications of the members were similar.[27]

Some of the counter arguments were stated by another judge:

> The only conceivable rationalization of this provision is that it is based on political units of the State and is analogous to the United States Senate. . . . The analogy cannot survive the most superficial

[27] Trial court in *Comm. for Fair Rep.* v. *Tawes* (1962), quoted in McKay, Robert, *Reapportionment and the Federal Analogy* (New York: National Municipal League, 1962), p. 4.

examination into the history of the requirement of the Federal Constitution and the diametrically opposing history of the requirements of the Alabama constitution that representation shall be based on population. Nor can it survive a comparison of the different political natures of states and counties.[28]

Space does not permit an examination of all the pros and cons.[29] Now, however, we are in a position to formulate a comprehensive description of the "federal plan": it is any deliberate apportionment of a legislature, usually of one chamber, in a manner calculated permanently to underrepresent urban or metropolitan people and a cluster of interest groups, and correspondingly to overrepresent the other people of a state by such devices as frozen districts, assignment of seats to local subdivisions or regions, or some area-population formula, in which the advantaged people and interest groups have virtually permanent control of the "federal" chamber, and often making it constitutionally the domain of one political party.

Conclusion

Baker v. *Carr* not only has shattered apportionments across the country, it also has led to fundamental reconsideration of our thought about representation. After generations of little thought or discussion about concepts of representation (except for city councils), the whole topic is reopened. Instead of trying to guess how much malrepresentation the courts may tolerate—the reflex to date of most legislatures—we should be discussing theories and devices of representation on a grand scale. There should be research on the effects and relative merits of single-member and multi-member districts, and consideration of systems of proportional representation. Surely some attention is due the unique and almost unnoticed Illinois cumulative voting device, which has demonstrated over a century its worth as an electoral-representation system, one that assures minority party representation in nearly every district,

[28] *Sims* v. *Frink,* 208 F. Supp. 431, 438 (1962).
[29] McKay, *op. cit.*

that averts the single-member district distortions, and mitigates sectional conflict.[30]

Thus far there has been a dearth of such thinking and discussion. One might say that the federal plans reflect creative thought, but they appear to be simply tactics by the groups which have long been overrepresented to hang on to their power. Any thought is mostly ex post facto rationalization. Indeed, the only bright spark of creative thought was the New Mexico weighted votes plan.[31] We long have insisted that our federal system affords fifty laboratories for innovation, but we have not done much experimenting in these laboratories.

[30] The system was conceived to mitigate sectional conflict and does it. With every district's three members split between the parties, party loyalty mitigates rather than exacerbates the sectional feeling.

[31] Credit belongs to Professor Frederick Irion, University of New Mexico, who conceived and sold the scheme.

☆ 15 ☆

PRINCIPLES FOR REAPPORTIONMENT: RECOMMENDATIONS

Advisory Commission on Intergovernmental Relations

The Commission is a permanent study and advisory group, composed of private citizens and local, state, and national officials, established by Congress to study the multifarious aspects of intergovernmental relations. Anticipating the momentous impact of Baker v. Carr, *the Commission made an intensive study of apportionment. Its report presents the following recommendations (some were not unanimous) as "principles for consideration and use by governors, legislators, and state and federal courts."*

The Commission's conclusions and recommendations, in the form of guiding principles to appropriate officials, can be broken down into three categories. The principles outlined in A through C relate to various procedures designed to facilitate periodic apportionment of seats in State legislatures. The principle contained in D is directed toward setting forth a firm boundary between judicial and political responsibilities. The permissible limits of a formula for the apportionment of State legislatures are contained in principle E.

Chapter V of *A Commission Report: Apportionment of State Legislatures* (December, 1962).

A. *Apportionment of seats in State legislative bodies is a basic factor of representative government in the United States and hence provisions relating thereto should be clearly specified in State constitutions.*

In order that State legislative bodies adequately reflect the needs and interests of the people of each individual State, each State should develop an apportionment formula that gives adequate representation to the diverse needs and interests of its people and at the same time satisfies the requirements imposed by the Fourteenth Amendment to the Constitution of the United States.

1. *The apportionment formula for each body of the State legislature should be spelled out in clear and sufficient detail so that there can be no question as to the meaning of the formula. The Commission recommends that, where a legislative body is to be apportioned according to population only, the State constitution specify the extent to which legislative districts may represent different numbers of people in terms of a percent deviation, not to exceed 10 percent, from the number obtained by dividing the total population of the State by the number of representatives in the legislative body.*

Regardless of what provisions are incorporated into the apportionment formulas of State constitutions, they should be clear enough that the apportioning body will have little difficulty in determining their application. Clarity is also necessary in order that the people may be in a position to evaluate the extent to which the apportioning body has met its responsibility and so that a court may easily decide if the State constitutional requirements have been complied with.

2. *The State constitution should specify the frequency of reapportionment.*

3. *The State constitution should specify the body or officer having a responsibility for apportioning seats in the State legislature. The Commission recommends that this responsibility be vested in the State legislature itself. It further recommends that a bipartisan or nonpartisan board or commission or other admin-*

istrative officer or body be given responsibility to apportion legislative seats if the legislature fails to act within the time specified by the constitution, or when the legislature acts in a manner which is subsequently declared unconstitutional by a court of competent jurisdiction.

State legislative bodies have found it extremely difficult to meet constitutional requirements calling for periodic apportionment of legislative seats. Periodic apportionment of legislative seats is based on the premise that population shifts or changes in other factors in apportionment formulas require a reallocation of legislative seats to reflect more accurately the changing needs and interests of the State as a whole. Yet an individual legislator has a responsibility to his constituency—he must protect its interests. In addition, supporting a proposal that would reduce the representation of his constituency might well eliminate him from the legislative body. While this may be a reasonable position for an individual State legislator, the cumulative effect of such action is to nullify, in whole or in part, a constitutional requirement for periodic apportionment of legislative seats.

In order to eliminate this type of avoidance of State constitutional provisions, the Commission urges all States to provide for a bipartisan or nonpartisan board or commission or other administrative officer or body to apportion seats in the State legislature in the event that the legislature itself fails to make the apportionment at the time stated in the constitution or if a court of competent jurisdiction has declared that a particular apportionment does not comply with the provisions of the State constitution.

B. *The people should have an opportunity at any time to react at the polls to the continuance or change of the formula apportioning seats in the State legislature.*

Constitutions are intended to provide a certain degree of stability to the institutions of the State. The provisions of State constitutions are designed to last for many years, but the constitutions are not intended to shackle future generations.

Several States, through use of the constitutional initiative, have been able to successfully meet this problem. However, there is no need for all States to adopt the constitutional initiative. The State constitution might provide that at specific intervals the question of the apportionment formula be placed on the ballot.

C. *The Commission recommends that State courts be constitutionally provided with appropriate jurisdiction and remedies to insure that State officials comply with their apportionment responsibilities.*

D. *The actual apportionment of a State legislature, including as it must, many elements of negotiation and accommodation that do not lend themselves to adversary proceedings, should be accomplished by the legislative or other specified nonjudicial body or officer. The Commission believes that State and Federal courts should confine their role to insuring that such nonjudicial body or officer promptly produce a reasonable apportionment meeting constitutional requirements, and urges both State and Federal courts to avoid, except in the most extreme circumstances, the prescription by judicial decree of specific apportionment formulas or the geographic composition of legislative districts.*

E. *Basis of apportionment.*

The preceding recommendations are directed toward improving the apportioning procedure. In the recommendation that follows, the Commission endeavors to resolve the question of the extent to which, if any, factors other than population may be used as the basis of apportionment. The Commission approaches this question not from the standpoint of constitutional law as such, but from the standpoint of legal, political, and philosophic needs of the nation.

"Equal protection of the laws" would seem to presume, and considerations of political equity demand, that the apportionment of both houses in the State legislature, be based strictly on population.

The Fourteenth Amendment to the United States Constitution is an amendment designed for the protection of the people. It is not intended to protect political subdivisions, minority views, or any particular form of governmental structure. The Fourteenth Amendment is concerned with one thing, and one thing only—that each person be treated equally in the eyes of the law of each and every State.

In applying the requirement that each person be treated equally in the eyes of State law to the question of apportionment of seats in the State legislature, only one interpretation is possible. That interpretation requires that each man's vote must count the same as every other man's vote. The State has no authority to classify people according to where they live—urban or rural areas—the type of work they do—laborer or banker—the type of education they have had—high school or college graduate—and authorize such classes to elect representatives to the State legislature in such a manner as to permit the vote of the members of any such class to have more weight in the election of State legislators than the members of any other class. Therefore, the Commission believes that population is the only fair and acceptable method of apportioning seats in the State legislature.

Assuming for the sake of discussion that the Fourteenth Amendment does not require the States to apportion solely on the basis of population, the history of representation in State legislatures and the theory of democratic government seem to demand that seats in State legislatures be apportioned according to population. The original constitutions of 36 States gave implicit recognition to this principle.

The government of the individual States is based on the theory of representative democracy. This means that legislative bodies must mirror the views of the citizens within the jurisdiction. This does not justify policy-making bodies being set up in such a way that minority interests of any type are represented in any way other than as justified by their relative numbers. They remain a minority interest until such time as they convince a majority of the people that their view is the one that should prevail. The fact that this permits a majority to impose its will on the minority is of no consequence. Our form of government is based on the assumption that a majority of the people elect a majority of the legislators to enact laws and develop policies that the voters have supported.

Except to the extent that they are represented according to their numbers and that they have an opportunity to present their views to that body, minorities are not entitled to protection in the State legislature. Protection of minority interests or views does not mean the minority should be in a position to veto the desires of the majority. The protection given minority views and interests should not be a veto power in the legislative process, since other adequate protections are offered by both Federal and State constitutions. If minority interests are permitted to control the legislative branch of State government so as to defeat the wishes of the majority, the nation is faced with one of three alternatives: (1) the eclipse of State government because the people will turn to a more broadly responsive National Government to obtain their needs; (2) the perpetuation of tyranny of a minority over the affairs of State government; or (3) the resort to precipitous or illegal means by the majority of the people whose desires have been frustrated.

The founders of this nation fully recognized that the nation and the States must be governed by the views of the majority of the voters. In enacting the Northwest Ordinance, the Congress affirmed the principle that representation in State and territorial legislatures was to be based on population. The new western States that entered the Union between 1790 and 1860 all apportioned seats in both houses of the State legislature according to population with but minor qualifications.

Some argue that the theory of checks and balances requires that if there are to be two houses of a legislature they must rest on different bases of apportionment. Obviously legislative bodies apportioned according to different formulas would be expected to consider issues in a different light. But this difference of viewpoint can be achieved even though both houses of a legislature are apportioned according to population. Members of the smaller legislative body would be responsible to a more diversified constituency. In addition, the term of members of one body could be longer than the term of the other and expire at different times.

Based on law—based on theory of democratic government—based on the history of representation in State government—the Commission reaches the inescapable conclusion that both houses of a State legislature should be apportioned strictly according to population.

PART V

Apportionment Standards

☆ 16 ☆

CONGRESSIONAL APPORTIONMENT: WESBERRY v. SANDERS

On February 17, 1964, two years after Baker, the Supreme Court held invalid the Georgia congressional districts because of population disparities. On the following opinion day, the Texas districts were ruled invalid. The table which follows this opinion indicates that the congressional districting patterns of several other states are vulnerable. Wesberry is likely to generate extensive litigation and redistricting. What about your state?

Here Colegrove was fully overruled and buried. The Court does not say why it chose to rest its decision on Article I, Section 2 rather than the equal protection clause. The following extract from the Court's decision omits the history of Article I, Section 2—the Federalist papers, the debates of the Constitutional Convention, and what transpired in the state ratifying conventions. Three justices (Harlan, Stewart, and Clark) read the history differently, and Justice Clark would have based the decision on the equal protection clause.

A Committee on Congress of the American Political Science Association recommended that the maximum variation in district population should be 15 percent of the mean. What standard does the Court prescribe?

MR. JUSTICE BLACK delivered the opinion of the Court.

Appellants are citizens and qualified voters of Fulton County, Georgia, and as such are entitled to vote in congressional elections

376 U.S. 1.

in Georgia's fifth congressional district. That district, one of ten created by a 1931 Georgia statute, includes Fulton, DeKalb, and Rockdale Counties and has a population according to the 1960 census of 823,680. The average population of the ten districts is 394,312, less than half that of the fifth. One district, the ninth, has only 272,154 people, less than one-third as many as the fifth. . . . The complaint alleged that appellants were deprived of the full benefit of their right to vote, in violation of (1) Art. I, § 2 of the Constitution of the United States, which provides that "The House of Representatives shall be composed of Members chosen every second year by the People of the several States . . ."; (2) the Due Process, Equal Protection, and Privileges and Immunities Clauses of the Fourteenth Amendment; and (3) that part of Section 2 of the Fourteenth Amendment which provides that "Representatives shall be apportioned among the several States according to their respective numbers. . . ."

The case was heard by a three-judge District Court, which found unanimously, from facts not disputed, that:

> It is clear by any standard . . . that the population of the Fifth District is grossly out of balance with that of the other nine congressional districts of Georgia and in fact, so much so that the removal of DeKalb and Rockdale Counties from the District, leaving only Fulton with a population of 556,326, would leave it exceeding the average by slightly more than forty percent.

Notwithstanding these findings, a majority of the court dismissed the complaint, citing as their guide Mr. Justice Frankfurter's minority opinion in *Colegrove* v. *Green,* 328 U.S. 549, an opinion stating that challenges to apportionment of congressional districts raised only "political" questions, which were not justiciable. . . . [In] debasing the weight of appellants' votes the State has abridged the right to vote for members of Congress guaranteed them by the United States Constitution. . . . The question of what relief should be given we leave for further consideration and decision by the District Court in light of existing circumstances. . . .

[The] statement in *Baker,* which referred to our past decisions holding congressional apportionment cases to be justiciable, we believe was wholly correct and we adhere to it. Mr. Justice Frankfurter's *Colegrove* opinion contended that Art. I, § 4, of the Constitution had given Congress "exclusive authority" to protect the right of citizens to vote for congressmen, but we made it clear in *Baker* that nothing in the language of that article gives support to a construction that would immunize state congressional apportionment laws which debase a citizen's right to vote from the power of courts to protect the constitutional rights of individuals from legislative destruction, a power recognized at least since our decision in *Marbury* v. *Madison,* 1 Cranch 137, in 1803. Cf. *Gibbons* v. *Ogden,* 9 Wheat. 1. The right to vote is too important in our free society to be stripped of judicial protection by such an interpretation of Article I. This dismissal can no more be justified on the ground of "want of equity" than on the ground of "non-justiciability." We therefore hold that the District Court erred in dismissing the complaint.

. . . We agree with the District Court that the 1931 Georgia apportionment grossly discriminates against voters in the fifth congressional district. A single congressman represents from two to three times as many fifth district voters as are represented by each of the congressmen from the other Georgia congressional districts. The apportionment statute thus contracts the value of some votes and expands that of others. If the federal constitution intends that when qualified voters elect members of Congress each vote be given as much weight as any other vote, then this statute cannot stand.

We hold that, construed in its historical context, the command of Art. I, § 2 that representatives be chosen "by the People of the several States" means that as nearly as is practicable one man's vote in a congressional election is to be worth as much as another's. This rule is followed automatically, of course, when representatives are chosen as a group on a statewide basis, as was a widespread practice in the first 50 years of our nation's history. It would be extraordinary to suggest that in such statewide elections the votes of inhabitants of some parts of a state, for example, Georgia's thinly populated ninth district, could be weighed at two or three times the value of the votes of people living in more populous parts of the state, for example, the fifth district around Atlanta. Cf. *Gray* v. *Sanders,* 372 U.S. 368. We do not believe that the framers of the Constitution intended to permit the same vote-diluting discrimination to be accomplished through the device of districts containing widely varied numbers of inhabitants. To say that a vote is worth more in one district than in another would not only run counter to our fundamental ideas of democratic government, it would cast aside the principle of a house of representatives elected by the People," a principle tenaciously fought for and established at the Constitutional Convention. The history of the Constitution, particularly that part of it relating to the adoption of Art. I, § 2, reveals that those who framed the Constitution meant that, no matter what the mechanics of an election, whether statewide or by districts, it was population which was to be the basis of the house of representatives. . . .

It is in the light of such history that we must construe Art. I, § 2, of the Constitution, which, carrying out the ideas of Madison and those of like views, provides that representatives shall be chosen "by the People of the several States" and shall be "apportioned among the several States . . . according to their respective numbers." It is not surprising that our court has held that this article gives persons qualified to vote a constitutional right to vote and to have their votes counted. . . . No right is more precious in a free country than that of having a voice in the election of those who make the laws under which, as good citizens, we must live. Other rights, even the most basic, are illusory if the right to vote is undermined. Our Constitution leaves no room for classification of people in a way that unnecessarily abridges this right. In urging the people to adopt the Constitution, Madison said in No. 57 of *The Federalist:*

Who are to be the electors of the Fœderal Representatives? Not the rich more than the poor; not the learned more than the ignorant; not

Variations in Populations of Congressional Districts
March 1, 1964. 43 States with Districts

State	Number of Districts	Largest District (000)	Smallest District (000)	Value vote Smallest District (Largest=1)	Average District Deviation	Deviating Over 15 Percent: Number	Deviating Over 15 Percent: Percent	Last Districting
Alabama	9	635	236	2.7	24.1%	5	56%	1931
Arizona	3	663	198	3.3	36.3	2	67	1961
Arkansas	4	575	333	1.7	22.4	4	100	1961
California	38	589	302	2.0	10.1	10	24	1961
Colorado	4	654	196	3.3	30.9	2	50	1921
Connecticut	5	690	319	2.2	25.9	4	80	1931
Florida	12	660	237	2.8	19.2	5	42	1961
Georgia	10	824	272	3.0	26.1	6	60	1931
Idaho	2	410	257	1.6	28.6	2	100	1911
Illinois	24	553	279	2.0	12.0	9	38	1961
Indiana	11	698	291	2.4	19.4	6	55	1941
Iowa	7	442	353	1.3	5.1		0	1961
Kansas	5	540	374	1.4	10.9	1	20	1961
Kentucky	7	611	351	1.7	28.9	4	57	1962
Louisiana	8	536	264	2.0	16.2	4	50	1912
Maine	2	505	464	1.1	4.3		0	1961
Maryland	7	711	244	2.9	44.9	6	86	1951
Massachusetts	12	479	376	1.3	6.3		0	1962
Michigan	19	490	306	1.6	9.2	3	16	1963
Minnesota	8	483	375	1.3	7.7		0	1961
Mississippi	5	608	295	2.1	19.4		60	1962
Missouri	10	507	378	1.3	8.5	1	10	1961
Montana	2	401	274	1.5	18.7	2	100	1917
Nebraska	3	531	405	1.3	9.3		0	1961
New Hampshire	2	332	275	1.2	7.0		0	1881
New Jersey	15	586	255	2.3	34.8	10	60	1961
New York	41	464	350	1.3	5.1		0	1961
North Carolina	11	491	278	1.8	12.7	4	36	1961
North Dakota	2	333	299	1.1	5.4		0	1961
Ohio	23	726	236	3.1	21.4	13	57	1951
Oklahoma	6	552	227	2.4	27.1	4	67	1951
Oregon	4	522	265	2.0	20.0	3	75	1941
Pennsylvania	27	553	303	1.8	10.4	9	33	1962
Rhode Island	2	460	400	1.2	7.0		0	1931
South Carolina	6	531	272	2.0	17.3	3	50	1932
South Dakota	2	498	183	2.7	46.3	2	100	1931
Tennessee	9	627	223	2.8	23.2	6	67	1951
Texas	22	952	216	4.4	34.0	19	86	1957
Utah	2	573	318	1.8	28.6	2	100	1931
Virginia	10	540	313	1.7	14.5	4	40	1952
Washington	7	511	343	1.5	8.6	2	29	1957
West Virginia	5	422	303	1.4	12.0	1	20	1961
Wisconsin	10	409	382	1.0	1.5	0	0	1963

Source: Howard D. Hamilton and Robert M. Howard, "Congressional Districting in Indiana," *Indiana Public Affairs Notes*, March-April, 1964.

the haughty heirs of distinguished names, more than the humble sons of obscure and unpropitious fortune. The electors are to be the great body of the people of the United States. . . .

Readers surely could have fairly taken this to mean, "one person, one vote." Cf. *Gray* v. *Sanders,* 372 U.S. 368,381.

While it may not be possible to draw congressional districts with mathematical precision, that is no excuse for ignoring our Constitution's plan objective of making equal representation for equal numbers of people the fundamental goal for the house of representatives. That is the high standard of justice and common sense which the founders set for us.

☆ *17* ☆

LEGISLATIVE APPORTIONMENT AND EQUAL PROTECTION OF THE LAWS: THE 1964 SUPREME COURT DECISIONS

Baker presaged substantial, even sweeping, redistribution of the keys to power in many states, but did not indicate the standards for apportionment betyond the obvious intimation that population should be a major criterion. Answers to many of the questions posed by Baker were furnished by the Court on June 15, 1964, in the six cases extracted below. The Court spoke decisively, ruling all six states' apportionments, including variations in Alabama and Delaware, unconstitutional.

The votes were 6-3 in the Colorado and New York cases, 7-2 in the Maryland case, and 8-1 in the Alabama, Delaware, and Virginia cases. The Chief Justice spoke—forthrightly and unambiguously—for himself and the same five associates. Justice Clark dissented in two cases and concurred in the others. Justice Stewart dissented in three and concurred in the rest. Justice Harlan dissented in all and filed a lengthy opinion stating his intense disagreement with the Court majority, and repeating the arguments made by him and Justice Frankfurter in Colegrove, Baker, and Wesberry. Thus the line-up was 6-3 on the Court's major proposition: that population must be the fundamental and controlling factor in apportionment of legislatures and of both chambers.

In the major opinion, the Alabama case, Reynolds v. Sims, the Court discussed issues of representation at length and went to great effort to formulate a comprehensive set of apportionment standards for the guidance of lower courts and legislatures. Because it rejected any mathematical formula, its verbal standards will acquire clarity and detail only when applied to concrete cases. Therefore it is informative to observe how the Court applied its newly announced standards to the facts of these six cases. The cases also shed light on the variety of apportionment arrangements, the extent of inequality prior to Baker, and the strategies adopted after Baker by status quo groups, e.g., in Delaware, Maryland, and Colorado.

By what chain of reasoning does the Court infer that equal districts are dictated by the Constitution? Which considerations other than population are permissible and which are impermissible? Why did the Court regard the federal analogy as "unimpressive" or specious? Was the Court's action in the Colorado case, and the others, consistent with democratic theory? Was it "interpretation," "judicial legislation," or "judicial usurpation"?

On June 22, 1964, the Court summarily held unconstitutional the apportionments of the legislatures in nine more states, on the basis of its decisions the previous week. These states are Connecticut, Florida, Idaho, Illinois, Iowa, Michigan, Ohio, Oklahoma, and Washington.

THE ALABAMA CASE: *Reynolds* v. *Sims*

MR. CHIEF JUSTICE WARREN delivered the opinion of the Court.

Involved in these cases are an appeal and two cross-appeals from a decision of the Federal District Court for the Middle District of Alabama holding invalid, under the Equal Protection Clause of the Federal Constitution, the existing and two legislatively proposed plans for the apportionment of seats in the two houses of the Alabama Legislature, and ordering into effect a temporary reappor-

377 U.S. 533.

tionment plan comprised of parts of the proposed but judicially disapproved measures. . . .

In *Baker* v. *Carr,* 369 U.S. 186, we held that a claim asserted under the Equal Protection Clause challenging the constitutionality of a state's apportionment of seats in its legislature, on the ground that the right to vote of certain citizens was effectively impaired since debased and diluted in effect, presented a justiciable controversy subject to adjudication by federal courts. The spate of similar cases filed and decided by lower courts since our decision in *Baker* amply shows that the problem of state legislative malapportionment is one that is perceived to exist in a large number of the States. . . .

In *Gray* v. *Sanders,* 372 U.S. 368, we held that the Georgia county unit system, applicable in statewide primary elections, was unconstitutional since it resulted in a dilution of the weight of the votes of certain Georgia voters merely because of where they resided. . . .

In *Wesberry* v. *Sanders,* 376 U.S. 1, decided earlier this term, we held that attacks on the constitutionality of congressional districting plans enacted by state legislatures do not present nonjusticiable questions and should not be dismissed generally for "want of equity." We determined that the constitutional test for the validity of congressional districting schemes was one of substantial equality of population among the various districts established by a state legislature for the election of members of the federal house of representatives.

. . . *Wesberry* clearly established that the fundamental principle of representative government in this country is one of equal representation for equal numbers of people, without regard to race, sex, economic status, or place of residence within a state. Our problem, then, is to ascertain, in the instant cases, whether there are any constitutionally cognizable principles which would justify departures from the basic standard of equality among voters in the apportionment of seats in state legislatures. . . .

Legislators represent people, not trees or acres. Legislators are elected by voters, not farms or cities or economic interests. As long as ours is a representative form of government, and our legislatures are those instruments of government elected directly by and directly representative of the people, the right to elect legislators in a free and unimpaired fashion is a bedrock of our political system. . . . And, if a state should provide that the votes of citizens in one part of the state should be given two times, or five times, or ten times the weight of votes of citizens in another part of the state, it could hardly be contended that the right to vote of those residing in the disfavored areas had not been effectively diluted. It would appear extraordinary to suggest that a state could be constitutionally permitted to enact a law providing that certain of the state's voters could vote 2, 5, or 10 times for their legislative representatives, while voters living elsewhere could vote only once. And it is inconceivable that a state law to the effect that, in counting votes for legislators, the votes of citizens in one part of the state would be multiplied by 2, 5, or 10, while the votes of persons in another area would be counted only at face value, could be constitutionally sustainable. . . . Weighting the votes of citizens differently, by any method or means, merely because of where they happen to reside, hardly seems justifiable. One must be ever aware that the Constitution forbids "sophisticated as well as simple-minded modes of discrimination." *Lane* v. *Wilson,* 307 U.S. 268, 275, *Gomillion* v. *Lightfoot*, 364 U.S. 339, 342. . . .

Logically, in a society ostensibly grounded on representative government, it would seem reasonable that a majority of the people of a state could elect a majority of that state's legislators. To conclude differently, and to sanction minority control of state legislative bodies, would appear to deny majority rights in a way that far surpasses any possible denial of minority rights that might otherwise be thought to result. Since legislatures are responsible for enacting laws by which all citizens are to be governed, they should be bodies which are collectively responsive to the popular will. And the concept of equal protection has been traditionally viewed as requiring the uniform treatment of persons standing in the same relation to the governmental action questioned or challenged. With respect to the allocation of legislative representation, all voters, as citizens of a state, stand in the same relation regardless of where they live.

Any suggested criteria for the differentiation of citizens are insufficient to justify any discrimination, as to the weight of their votes, unless relevant to the permissible purposes of legislative apportionment. Since the achieving of fair and effective representation for all citizens is concededly the basic aim of legislative apportionment, we conclude that the Equal Protection Clause guarantees the opportunity for equal participation by all voters in the election of state legislators. . . . Our constitutional system amply provides for the protection of minorities by means other than giving them majority control of state legislatures.

We are told that the matter of apportioning representation in a state legislature is a complex and many-faceted one. We are advised that states can rationally consider factors other than population in apportioning legislative representation. We are admonished not to restrict the power of the states to impose differing views as to political philosophy on their citizens. We are cautioned about the dangers of entering into political thickets and mathematical quagmires. Our answer is this: a denial of constitutionally protected rights demands judicial protection; our oath and our office require no less of us. As stated in *Gomillion* v. *Lightfoot, supra:* "When a State exercises power wholly within the domain of state interest, it is insulated from federal judicial review. But such insulation is not carried over when state power is used as an instrument for circumventing a federally protected right." To the extent that a citizen's right to vote is debased, he is that much less a citizen. The fact that an individual lives here or there is not a legitimate reason for overweighting or diluting the efficacy of his vote. The complexions of societies and civilizations change, often with amazing rapidity. A nation once primarily rural in character becomes predominantly urban. Representation schemes once fair and equitable become archaic and outdated. But the basic principle of representative government remains, and must remain, unchanged—the weight of a citizen's vote cannot be made to depend on where he lives. Population is, of necessity, the starting point for consideration and the controlling criterion for judgment in legislative apportionment controversies. . . .

IV.

We hold that, as a basic constitutional standard, the Equal Protection Clause requires that the seats in both houses of a bicameral state legislature must be apportioned on a population basis. Simply stated, an individual's right to vote for state legislators is unconstitutionally impaired when its weight is in a substantial fashion diluted when compared with votes of citizens living in other parts of the state. Since, under neither the existing apportionment provisions nor under either of the proposed plans was either of the houses of the Alabama Legislature apportioned on a population basis, the District Court correctly held that all three of these schemes were constitutionally invalid. . . .

[The Federal Analogy]

Since neither of the houses of the Alabama Legislature, under any of the three plans considered by the District Court, was apportioned on a population basis, we would be justified in proceeding no further. However, one of the proposed plans, that contained in the so-called 67-Senator Amendment, at least superficially resembles the scheme of legislative representation followed in the federal Congress. Under this plan, each of Alabama's 67 counties is alloted one senator, and no counties are given more than one senate seat. Arguably, this is analogous to the allocation of two senate seats, in the federal Congress, to each of the 50 states, regardless of population. Seats in the Alabama House, under the proposed constitutional amendment, are distributed by giving each of the 67 counties at least one, with the remaining 39 seats being allotted among the more populous counties on a population basis. This scheme, at least at first glance, appears to resemble that prescribed for the federal house of representatives, where the 435 seats are distributed among the states on a population basis, although each state, regardless of its population, is given at least one congressman. Thus, although there are substantial differences in underlying rationale and result, the 67-Senator Amendment, as proposed by the

Alabama Legislature, at least arguably presents for consideration a scheme analogous to that used for apportioning seats in Congress.

Much has been written since our decision in *Baker* v. *Carr* about the applicability of the so-called federal analogy to state legislative apportionment arrangements. . . . We find the federal analogy inapposite and irrelevant to state legislative districting schemes. Attempted reliance on the federal analogy appears often to be little more than an after-the-fact rationalization offered in defense of maladjusted state apportionment arrangements. The original constitutions of 36 of our states provided that representation in both houses of the state legislatures would be based completely, or predominantly, on population. And the Founding Fathers clearly had no intention of establishing a pattern or model for the apportionment of seats in state legislatures when the system of representation in the federal Congress was adopted. Demonstrative of this is the fact that the Northwest Ordinance, adopted in the same year, 1787, as the federal constitution, provided for the apportionment of seats in territorial legislatures solely on the basis of population.

The system of representation in the two houses of the federal Congress is one ingrained in our Constitution, as part of the law of the land. It is one conceived out of compromise and concession indispensable to the establishment of our federal republic. Arising from unique historical circumstances, it is based on the consideration that in establishing our type of federalism a group of formerly independent states bound themselves together under one national government. Admittedly, the original 13 states surrendered some of their sovereignty in agreeing to join together "to form a more perfect Union." But at the heart of our constitutional system remains the concept of separate and distinct governmental entities which have delegated some, but not all, of their formerly held powers to the single national government. . . .

Political subdivisions of states—counties, cities, or whatever—never were and never have been considered as sovereign entities. Rather, they have been traditionally regarded as subordinate governmental instrumentalities created by the state to assist in the carrying out of state governmental functions. As stated by the Court in *Hunter* v. *City of Pittsburgh*, 207 U.S. 161, 178, these governmental units are "created as convenient agencies for exercising such of the governmental powers of the state as may be entrusted to them," and the "number, nature, and duration of the powers conferred upon [them] . . . and the territory over which they shall be exercised rests in the absolute discretion of the state." The relationship of the states to the federal government could hardly be less analogous. . . .

Since we find the so-called federal analogy inapposite to a consideration of the constitutional validity of state legislative apportionment schemes, we necessarily hold that the Equal Protection Clause requires both houses of a state legislature to be apportioned on a population basis. The right of a citizen to equal representation and to have his vote weighted equally with those of all other citizens in the election of members of one house of a bicameral state legislature would amount to little if states could effectively submerge the equal-population principle in the apportionment of seats in the other house. If such a scheme were permissible, an individual citizen's ability to exercise an effective voice in the only instrument of state government directly representative of the people might be almost as effectively thwarted as if neither house were apportioned on a population basis. Deadlock between the two bodies might result in compromise and concession on some issues. But in all too many cases the more probable result would be frustration of the majority will through minority veto in the house not apportioned on a population basis, stemming directly from the failure to accord adequate overall legislative representation to all of the state's citizens on a nondiscriminatory basis. In summary, we can perceive no constitutional difference, with respect to the geographical distribution of state legislative representation, between the two houses of a bicameral state legislature.

We do not believe that the concept of bicameralism is rendered anachronistic and meaningless when the predominant basis of representation in the two state legislative bodies is required to be the same—population. A prime reason for bicameralism, modernly considered, is to insure mature and deliberate consideration of, and to prevent precipitate action on, proposed legislative measures. Simply because the controlling criterion for apportioning representation is required to be the same in both houses does not mean that there will be no differences in the composition and complexion of the two bodies. . . .

By holding that as a federal constitutional requisite both houses of a state legislature must be apportioned on a population basis, we mean that the Equal Protection Clause requires that a state make an honest and good faith effort to construct districts, in both houses of its legislature, as nearly of equal population as is practicable. We realize that it is a practical impossibility to arrange legislative districts so that each one has an identical number of residents, or citizens, or voters. Mathematical exactness or precision is hardly a workable constitutional requirement.

. . . Lower courts can and assuredly will work out more concrete and specific standards for evaluating state legislative apportionment schemes in the context of actual litigation. For the present, we deem it expedient not to attempt to spell out any precise constitutional tests. What is marginally permissible in one state may be unsatisfactory in another, depending on the particular circumstances of the case. Developing a body of doctrine on a case-by-case basis appears to us to provide the most satisfactory means of arriving at detailed constitutional requirements in the area of state legislative apportionment. Thus, we proceed to state here only a few rather general considerations which appear to us to be relevant.

A state may legitimately desire to maintain the integrity of various political subdivisions, insofar as possible, and provide for compact districts of contiguous territory in designing a legislative apportionment scheme. Valid considerations may underlie such aims. Indiscriminate districting, without any regard for political subdivision or natural or historical boundary lines, may be little more than an open invitation to partisan gerrymandering. Single-member districts may be the rule in one state, while another state might desire to achieve some flexibility by creating multimember or floterial districts. Whatever the means of accomplishment, the overriding objective must be substantial equality of population among the various districts, so that the vote of any citizen is approximately equal in weight to that of any other citizen in the state.

History indicates, however, that many states have deviated, to a greater or lesser degree, from the equal-population principle in the apportionment of seats in at least one house of their legislatures. So long as the divergences from a strict population standard are based on legitimate considerations incident to the effectuation of a rational state policy, some deviations from the equal-population principle are constitutionally permissible with respect to the apportionment of seats in either or both of the two houses of a bicameral state legislature. But neither history alone, nor economic or other sorts of group interests, are permissible factors in attempting to justify disparities from population-based representation. Citizens, not history or economic interests, cast votes. Considerations of area alone provide an insufficient justification for deviations from the equal-population principle. Again, people, not land or trees or pastures, vote. Modern developments and improvements in transportation and communications make rather hollow, in the mid-1960's, most claims that deviations from population-based representation can validly be based solely on geographical considerations. Arguments for allowing such deviations in order to insure effective representation for sparsely settled areas and to prevent legislative districts from becoming so large that the availability of access of citizens to their representatives is impaired are today, for the most part, unconvincing.

VIII.

That the Equal Protection Clause requires that both houses of a state legislature be apportioned on a population basis does not mean that states cannot adopt some reasonable plan for periodic revision of their apportionment schemes. Decennial reapportionment appears to be a rational approach to readjustment of legislative representation in order to take into account population shifts and growth. Reallocation of legislative seats every ten years coincides with the prescribed practice in 41 of the states, often honored more in the breach than the observance, however. . . . [W]e do not mean to intimate that more frequent reapportionment would not be constitutionally permissible or practically desirable. But if reapportionment were accomplished with less frequency, it would assuredly be constitutionally suspect.

X.

We do not consider here the difficult question of the proper remedial devices which federal courts should utilize in state legislative apportionment cases. Remedial technique in this new and developing area of the law will probably often differ with the circumstances of the challenged apportionment and a variety of local conditions. It is enough to say now that, once a state's legislative apportionment scheme has been found to be unconstitutional, it would be the unusual case in which a court would be justified in not taking appropriate action to insure that no further elections are conducted under the invalid plan. However, under certain circumstances, such as where an impending election is imminent and a state's election machinery is already in progress, equitable considerations might justify a court in withholding the granting of immediately effective relief in a legislative apportionment case, even though the existing apportionment scheme was found invalid. In awarding or withholding immediate relief, a court is entitled to and should consider the proximity of a forthcoming election and the mechanics and complexities of state election laws, and should act and rely upon general equitable principles.

THE COLORADO CASE: *Lucas* v. *Colorado General Assembly*

MR. CHIEF JUSTICE WARREN delivered the opinion of the Court. . . .

At the November 1962 general election, the Colorado electorate adopted proposed Amendment No. 7 by a vote of 305,700 to

377 U.S. 713.

172,725, and defeated proposed Amendment No. 8 by a vote of 311,749 to 149,822. Amendment No. 8, rejected by a majority of the voters, prescribed an apportionment plan pursuant to which seats in both houses of the Colorado Legislature would purportedly be apportioned on a population basis. Amendment No. 7, on the other hand, provided for the apportionment of the House of Representatives on the basis of population, but essentially maintained the existing apportionment in the Senate, which was based on a combination of population and various other factors.

Plaintiffs requested a declaration that Amendment No. 7 was unconstitutional under the Fourteenth Amendment since resulting in substantial disparities from population-based representation in the Senate, and asked for a decree reapportioning both houses of the Colorado Legislature on a population basis.

Several aspects of this case serve to distinguish it from the other cases involving state legislative apportionment also decided this date. Initially, one house of the Colorado Legislature is at least arguably apportioned substantially on a population basis under Amendment No. 7 and the implementing statutory provisions. Under the apportionment schemes challenged in the other cases, on the other hand, clearly neither of the houses in any of the state legislatures is apportioned sufficiently on a population basis so as to be constitutionally sustainable. Additionally, the Colorado scheme of legislative apportionment here attacked is one adopted by a majority vote of the Colorado electorate almost contemporaneously with the District Court's decision on the merits in this litigation. Thus, the plan at issue did not result from prolonged legislative inaction. However, the Colorado General Assembly, in spite of the state constitutional mandate for periodic reapportionment, has enacted only one effective legislative apportionment measure in the past 50 years.

Finally, this case differs from the others decided this date in that the iniative device provides a practicable political remedy to obtain relief against alleged legislative malapportionment in Colorado. An initiated measure proposing a constitutional amendment or a statutory enactment is entitled to be placed on the ballot if the signatures of 8 percent of those voting for the secretary of state in the last election are obtained.

Except as an interim remedial procedure justifying a court in staying its hand temporarily, we find no significance in the fact that a nonjudicial, political remedy may be available for the effectuation of asserted rights to equal representation in a state legislature. Courts sit to adjudicate controversies involving alleged denials of constitutional rights. While a court sitting as a court of equity might be justified in temporarily refraining from the issuance of injunctive relief in an apportionment case in order to allow for resort to an available political remedy, such an iniative and referendum, individual constitutional rights cannot be deprived, or denied judicial effectuation, because of the existence of a nonjudicial remedy through which relief against the alleged malapportionment, which the individual voters seek, might be achieved. An individual's constitutionally protected right to cast an equally weighted vote cannot be denied even by a vote of a majority of a state's electorate, if the apportionment scheme adopted by the voters fails to measure up to the requirements of the Equal Protection Clause. Manifestly, the fact that an apportionment plan is adopted in a popular referendum is insufficient to sustain its constitutionality or to induce a court of equity to refuse to act. As stated by this Court in *West Virginia State Bd. of Educ.* v. *Barnette,* 319 U.S. 624, 638, "One's right to life, liberty, and property . . . and the other fundamental rights may not be submitted to vote; they depend on the outcome of no elections." A citizen's constitutional rights can hardly be infringed simply because a majority of the people choose to do so. We hold that the fact that a challenged legislative apportionment plan was approved by the electorate is without federal constitutional significance, if the scheme adopted fails to satisfy the basic requirements of the Equal Protection Clause, as delineated in our opinion in *Reynolds* v. *Sims*. And we conclude that the fact that a practicably available political remedy, such as initiative and referendum, exists under state law provides justification only for a court of equity to stay its hand temporarily while recourse to such a remedial device is attempted or while proposed initiated measures relating to legislative apportionment are pending and will be submitted to the state's voters at the next election. . . .

THE DELAWARE CASE: *Roman* v. *Sincock*

MR. CHIEF JUSTICE WARREN delivered the opinion of the Court. . . .

Plaintiffs below alleged that the apportionment of seats in the Delaware Legislature resulted in an "invidious discrimination as to the inhabitants of New Castle County and the City of Wilmington," operated to deny them the right to cast votes for Delaware legislators "that are of equal effect with that of every other citizen of the State of Delaware," and was arbitrary and capricious in failing to provide a reasonable classification of those voting for members of the Delaware General Assembly. Plaintiffs also asserted that they were without any other adequate remedy since the existing legislative apportionment was frozen into the 1897 Delaware Constitution; that the present legislature was dominated by legislators representing the two less populous counties; that it was, as a practical matter, impossible to amend the state constitution or convene a constitutional convention for the purpose of reapportioning the General Assembly; and that the Delaware Legislature had consistently failed to take appropriate action with respect to reapportionment. . . .

Under the 1897 apportionment scheme, as perpetuated over 65 years later, senate districts ranged in population from 4,177 to 64,820, resulting in a maximum population-variance ratio, between the most populous and least populous senate districts, of about 15 to 1.

Representative districts ranged in population, as of 1960, from 1,643 to 58,228, under Art. II § 2, of the 1897 Delaware Constitution, resulting in a maximum population-variance ratio, in the Delaware House, of about 35 to 1. . . .

Under the 1963 amendment to Art. II, § 2, of the Delaware

377 U.S. 695.

Constitution, the size of the senate is increased from 17 to 21 members. . . . Under the revised apportionment, the maximum population-variance ratio is reduced to about 12 to 1 with respect to the house, but remains about 15 to 1 in the senate.

The 1963 amendment also provided that, if a constitutional convention were to be called, the number of delegates and the method of their election were not to be affected by the amended apportionment provisions, and, for the purpose of any future constitutional convention, the representative districts were to elect delegates on the basis of the apportionment provided by Art. II, § 2, as it existed prior to the amendment. Thus, the number of constitutional convention delegates would continue to be 41, one from each of the 35 representative districts provided for under the 1897 scheme, with two elected at large from each of the three counties.

In *Reynolds* v. *Sims,* ___ U.S. ___, decided also this date, we held that the Equal Protection Clause requires that seats in both houses of a bicameral state legislature must be apportioned substantially on a population basis. Neither of the houses of the Delaware General Assembly, either before or after the 1963 constitutional amendment, was so apportioned. Thus, we hold that the District Court correctly found the Delaware legislative apportionment constitutionally invalid, and affirm the decisions below.

THE MARYLAND CASE: *Maryland Committee* v. *Tawes*

MR. CHIEF JUSTICE WARREN delivered the opinion of the Court. . . .

Under Art. III, § 2, of the Maryland Constitution, each of the state's 23 counties is allocated one seat in the Maryland senate, and each of the six legislative districts of the City of Baltimore is also entitled to one senate seat—resulting in a total of 29 seats in the Maryland senate. . . . A maximum population-variance ratio of almost 32 to 1 exists between the most populous and least populous counties. . . .

377 U.S. 656.

Under the existing house apportionment, [a] maximum population-variance ratio of over 12 to 1 existed between the most populous and least populous counties. Baltimore County, with a 1960 population of 492,428, had only the same number of house seats, six, as did Garrett and Somerset counties, whose combined 1960 population was 40,043.

Under the 1962 temporary legislation reapportioning the Maryland House of Delegates, the only practical effect is to add 19 house seats. . . . Under the new legislation, [a] maximum population-variance ratio of almost 6 to 1 still exists between the most populous and least populous house districts. . . .

Neither in the Maryland Constitution nor in the state statutes is there any provision relating to the reapportionment of representation in the General Assembly. Apart from the limited and temporary reapportionment of the house enacted at the 1962 special session of the Maryland Legislature, following the holding of the Circuit Court that the house apportionment provisions of the Maryland Constitution were invalid, all efforts since 1867 to achieve a substantial reapportionment of seats in the General Assembly, with two rather minor exceptions, have been futile. . . .

Regardless of possible concessions made by the parties and the scope of the consideration of the courts below, in reviewing a state legislative apportionment case this court must of necessity consider the challenged scheme as a whole in determining whether the particular state's apportionment plan, in its entirety, meets federal constitutional requisites. It is simply impossible to decide upon the validity of the apportionment of one house of a bicameral legislature in the abstract, without also evaluating the actual scheme of representation employed with respect to the other house. Rather, the proper, and indeed indispensable, subject for judicial focus in a legislative apportionment controversy is the overall representation accorded to the state's voters, in both houses of a bicameral state legislature. We therefore reject appellees' contention that the Court is precluded from considering the validity of the apportionment of the Maryland House of Delegates. . . .

In *Reynolds* v. *Sims,* ___ U.S. ___, decided also this date, we held that seats in both houses of a bicameral state legislature are required, under the Equal Protection Clause, to be apportioned substantially on a population basis. Neither house of the Maryland Legislature, even after the 1962 legislation reapportioning the House of Delegates, is apportioned sufficiently on a population basis to be constitutionally sustainable. . . .

THE NEW YORK CASE: *WMCA* v. *Lomenzo*

MR. CHIEF JUSTICE WARREN delivered the opinion of the Court. . . .

The result of applying [the] complicated apportionment formula is to give the populous counties markedly less senatorial representation, when compared with respective population figures, than the less populous counties. Under the 1953 apportionment, based on the 1950 census, a senator from one of the less populous counties represented, on the average, 195,859 citizens, while a senator from a populous county represented an average of 301,178. Under the pending apportionment based on the 1960 census, the average population of the senatorial districts in the populous counties will be 366,128. On the other hand, the average population of the senatorial districts in the less populous counties, is only 216,822. Thus, a citizen in a less populous county had, under the 1953 apportionment, over 1.5 times the representation, on the average, of a citizen in a populous county, and, under the apportionment based on the 1960 census, this ratio will be about 1.7 to 1.

With respect to the Assembly, the six assemblymen currently elected from Nassau County represent an average citizen population of 212,634, and one of that county's current Assembly districts has a citizen population of 314,721. Suffolk County's three assemblymen presently represent an average of 216,704 citizens. On the other hand, the least populous Assembly district, Schuyler County, has a citizen population, according to the 1960 census, of only

377 U.S. 633.

14,974, and yet, in accordance with the constitutional formula, is allocated one Assembly seat. Under the new apportionment, Schuyler County will again be given one assembly seat, while one projected Monroe County district will have a citizen population of 190,343 and an Assembly district in Suffolk County will have over 170,000 citizens. Additionally, the average population of the 54 Assembly districts in New York City's four populous counties will be in excess of 132,000 citizens each.

. . . Neither house of the New York Legislature, under the state constitutional formulas and the implementing statutory provisions here attacked, is presently or, when reapportioned on the basis of 1960 census figures, will be apportioned sufficiently on a population basis to be constitutionally sustainable. Accordingly, we hold that the District Court erred in upholding the constitutionality of New York's scheme of legislative apportionment. . . .

THE VIRGINIA CASE: *Davis* v. *Mann*

MR. CHIEF JUSTICE WARREN delivered the opinion of the Court. . . .

Section 24–14 of the Virginia Code, as amended in 1962, provides for the apportionment of the Virginia senate, and divides the state into 36 senatorial districts for the allocation of the 40 seats in that body. With a total state population of 3,966,949, according to the 1960 census, and 40 senate seats, the ideal ratio would be one senator for each 99,174 persons. Under the 1962 statute, however, Arlington County is given but one senator for its 163,401 persons, only .61 of the representation to which it would be entitled on a strict population basis. The City of Norfolk has only .65 of its ideal share of senatorial representation, with two senators for a population of 305,872. And Fairfax County (including the cities of Fairfax and Falls Church), with two senators for 285,194 people, has but .70 of its ideal representation in the Virginia senate. In comparison, the smallest senatorial district, with respect

377 U.S. 678.

to population, has only 61,730, and the next smallest 63,703. Thus, the maximum population-variance ratio between the most populous and least populous senatorial districts is 2.65 to 1. Under the 1962 senatorial apportionment, applying 1960 population figures, approximately 41.1 percent of the state's total population reside in districts electing a majority of the members of that body.

Apportionment of seats in the Virginia House of Delegates is provided for in § 24–12 of the Virginia Code, as amended in 1962, which creates 70 house districts and distributes the 100 house seats among them. Dividing the state's total 1960 population by 100 results in an ideal ratio of one delegate for each 39,669 persons. Fairfax County, with a population of 285,194, is allocated only three house seats under the 1962 apportionment provisions, however, thus being given only .42 of its ideal representation. While the average population per delegate in Fairfax County is 95,064, Wythe County, with only 21,975 persons, and Shenandoah County, with a population of only 21,825, are each given one seat in the Virginia house. The maximum population-variance ratio, between the most populous and least populous house districts, is thus 4.36 to 1. . . .

We reject appellants' argument that the underrepresentation of Arlington, Fairfax, and Norfolk is constitutionally justifiable since it allegedly resulted in part from the fact that those areas contain large numbers of military and military-related personnel. Discrimination against a class of individuals, merely because of the nature of their employment, without more being shown, is constitutionally impermissible. . . .

We also reject appellants' claim that the Virginia apportionment is sustainable as involving an attempt to balance urban and rural power in the legislature. Not only does this explanation lack legal merit, but it also fails to conform to the facts. Some Virginia urban areas, such as Richmond, by comparison with Arlington, Fairfax, and Norfolk, appear to be quite adequately represented in the General Assembly.

In *Reynolds* v. *Sims,* ___ U.S. ___, decided also this date, we held that the Equal Protection Clause requires that seats in both houses of a bicameral state legislature must be apportioned substantially on a population basis. Neither of the houses of the Virginia General Assembly, under the 1962 statutory provisions here attacked, is apportioned sufficiently on a population basis to be constitutionally sustainable. Accordingly, we hold that the District Court properly found the Virginia legislative apportionment invalid. . . .

☆ Appendix ☆

STATE-BY-STATE SUMMARY OF LEGISLATIVE APPORTIONMENT [AS OF MAY, 1964]

Charles S. Rhyne

On June 15, 1964, the Supreme Court decided six cases involving state legislative reapportionments; these cases are excerpted in Chapter 17, beginning on page 133. On June 22, 1964, the Court remanded nine more cases with instructions to decide them in accordance with the principles the Court set forth in the six cases of June 15. Included were cases from Connecticut, Florida, Idaho, Illinois, Iowa, Michigan, Ohio, Oklahoma, and Washington. In the following tabulation, an asterisk (*) marks the fifteen states covered by the actions of the Court on June 15 and 22.

There are five states in which state court actions are pending relating to legislative reapportionment (Michigan, Missouri, Nevada, New Jersey, and Pennsylvania); nineteen states in which court actions have been decided (California, Idaho, Illinois, Indiana, Kansas, Louisiana, Maryland, Massachusetts, Michigan, Minnesota, Mississippi, Missouri, New Hampshire, New Mexico, Rhode Island, Vermont, Virginia, West Virginia, Wisconsin); fifteen states in which federal court actions are pending (California, Connecticut, Idaho, Iowa, Kentucky, Michigan, Missouri, Nevada, New Hampshire, North Dakota, Pennsylvania, Rhode Island, Texas, Vermont, Wyoming); eighteen states in which federal court actions have been decided (Alabama, Colorado, Delaware, Florida, Georgia, Illinois, Indiana, Iowa, Nebraska, New Mexico, New York, Ohio, Oklahoma, Pennsylvania, Tennessee, Virginia, Washington, Wyoming). In at least thirty-eight states state or federal court actions have been either instituted or decided (Alabama, California, Colorado, Connecticut, Delaware, Florida, Georgia, Idaho, Illinois, Indiana, Iowa, Kansas, Kentucky, Louisiana, Maine, Maryland, Massachusetts, Michi-

gan, Mississippi, Missouri, Nebraska, Nevada, New Hampshire, New Jersey, New Mexico, New York, North Dakota, Ohio, Oklahoma, Rhode Island, Tennessee, Texas, Vermont, Virginia, Washington, West Virginia, Wisconsin, and Wyoming).

In five states legislative or constitutional action pertaining to reapportionment has been taken not directly pursuant to court order (Hawaii, two senate districts; Maine, house; North Carolina, house and senate; Pennsylvania, house and senate; Utah, house and senate). In forty-two states judicial, legislative, or constitutional action is pending or has been consummated (Alabama, California, Colorado, Connecticut, Delaware, Florida, Georgia, Hawaii, Idaho, Illinois, Indiana, Iowa, Kansas, Kentucky, Louisiana, Maine, Maryland, Massachusetts, Michigan, Mississippi, Missouri, Nebraska, Nevada, New Hampshire, New Jersey, New Mexico, New York, North Carolina, North Dakota, Ohio, Oklahoma, Pennsylvania, Rhode Island, Tennessee, Texas, Utah, Vermont, Virginia, Washington, West Virginia, Wisconsin, Wyoming).

Some of the legal issues facing the courts as a result of the more recent apportionment cases are as follows: (1) the validity of the so-called "little federal plan"; (2) the degree of malapportionment required in order to constitute "invidious discrimination" and thereby violate the Fourteenth Amendment, and whether the "one man-one vote" principle is to govern in this area; and (3) whether it is proper for courts to overrule apportionments which have been approved by initiative or referendum.

*Alabama

A "little federal plan" was struck down by a federal court. The case is now pending before the U.S. Supreme Court. The federal court indicated that population and not geographic area should be the basic consideration in representation in both houses.

Alaska

In 1961, prior to *Baker* v. *Carr*, the house was reapportioned without court order. The present senate apportionment scheme favors the rural areas.

Arizona

No action has been taken by either courts or legislature. The house districts are slightly weighted to the rural areas, as are the senate districts.

Arkansas

The Arkansas Supreme Court, just prior to *Baker* v. *Carr,* overruled the Arkansas Board of Apportionment and directly reapportioned the house. No court action has been initiated against the senate, the composition of which favors the rural areas.

California

The 1961 legislature reapportioned the senate under the current provisions of the state constitution, which limit each county to one senator. On August 20, 1963, the California Supreme Court unanimously dismissed a reapportionment suit demanding the reapportionment of the senate on a population basis. A suit is pending in a federal court concerning the proper apportionment of the senate. The house is apportioned according to population.

*Colorado

A federal court in July, 1963, held that the "little federal plan" apportionment formula, approved by the voters of the state in a 1962 referendum, was constitutional. An appeal challenging the federal court's ruling is now before the U.S. Supreme Court.

*Connecticut

A federal three-man court in July, 1964, ordered into effect a scheme to produce a new apportionment of the state senate and house, but the governor has asked the court to permit him to file an alternative plan which he claims would be more equitable and less costly.

*DELAWARE

A federal court has held that both houses of the legislature must be reapportioned according to population. An appeal is currently pending in the U.S. Supreme Court.

*FLORIDA

The senate and house were reapportioned by legislative act in 1963, which provides that the senate would consist of 43 members to be apportioned among the several counties of the state to provide equitable representation based upon similar economic interests, geographic area, and population. The house would consist of 112 representatives apportioned among the counties, each county having one representative and the remaining representative to be assigned to the counties in proportion to population. A federal court decision upholding this legislative reapportionment has been appealed to the U.S. Supreme Court.

GEORGIA

A federal court in 1962 ruled that apportionment of the legislature amounted to "invidious discrimination" and ordered the state to reapportion "at least one" of the houses of the legislature on a population basis. Subsequently, the legislature passed a bill reapportioning the senate along population lines. Special elections were ordered to fill new urban-area seats for the 1963 legislative session. The legislature also placed on the November ballot a constitutional amendment requiring that senators from multi-member counties all be elected on a county-wide basis. The amendment was approved. However, a federal court has held the county unit system invalid. An appeal is pending before the U.S. Supreme Court.

HAWAII

The state's apportionment, weighted to the Outer Islands so that Honolulu will not dominate the state's government, has not been subjected to court challenge since statehood was achieved. In 1962 voters approved a minor amendment changing borders of two senate districts.

*IDAHO

On May 8, 1962, the Idaho Supreme Court held that apportionment of the house did not violate the U.S. Constitution. The house apportionment guarantees one representative to every county. The legislature has passed a limited reapportionment measure. The size of the house has been increased from 62 to 79 members, but counties with as few as 910 residents still have a representative, and the rule of one senator to a county remained unchanged. A presession lawsuit in a federal court seeking greater equity than this was not dismissed. And the plaintiffs therein, citing the 1963 session's efforts as inadequate, are redoubling their demands in the federal court for judicial intervention.

*ILLINOIS

See preceding pages 104 to 107.

INDIANA

Reapportionment legislation was enacted in February, 1963, affecting the composition of both houses. This legislation was vetoed by the governor. However, the veto was upset by the Indiana Supreme Court on February 10, 1962, due to a technicality in the governor's exercise thereof. This legislative enactment utilized the 1960 federal census as an enumeration of all inhabitants over 21 years of age. This is now law and applicable to the 1964 general election.

Prior to the Indiana Supreme Court decision a federal court had ruled that a 1921 apportionment act was invidiously discriminatory and in violation of the U.S. Constitution. The Court then enjoined the conducting of any election to the Indiana General Assembly after the general election in 1964. It may well be that the effect of the federal court decision may be moot since the Indiana Supreme Court upheld the 1963 reapportionment act after this decision, thus repealing the 1921 Act with which the federal court was concerned.

*IOWA

A federal court has found the present Iowa apportionment to be invidiously discriminatory and has ordered reapportionment of the legislature. The federal court decision followed the defeat at the polls of a proposed constitutional amendment, the so-called "Shaff Plan," which would have provided a senate based on population and a house based on area. Justice White of the Supreme Court has declined to stay the federal court's ruling. The legislature complied with the federal court order by passing in special session a reapportionment plan that provides for sharply increased representation of populous counties in both houses.

KANSAS

In 1961 an act was enacted which reapportioned the house. This law was declared invalid by the Kansas Supreme Court. In 1963, legislation was enacted reapportioning the senate. This enactment was likewise declared invalid by the same court. In 1964 statutes were enacted reapportioning both the senate and the house so as to reflect population more accurately.

KENTUCKY

The Kentucky legislature was reapportioned by an extraordinary session effective February 28, 1963. Both houses were reapportioned by this session. While the state constitution requires that both houses be apportioned on a population basis, this standard was not strictly adhered to by the legislature in the enactment of the above legislation.

There is presently pending in a federal court an action filed June 26, 1962, seeking reapportionment of the Kentucky legislature. It was as a result of this action that the governor called the legislature into extraordinary session in January, 1963, for the purpose of reapportioning the legislature. When the legislature failed to allot to the urban areas the representation required by the state constitution, the complaint in the federal court was amended demanding that the legislature adhere to the provisions of the state constitution. No further action has been taken. It is anticipated that when the U.S. Supreme Court renders a decision in the apportionment cases now pending before it, this federal court litigation will be disposed of accordingly.

LOUISIANA

In June, 1963, a special session of the legislature approved a new population-based house apportionment plan. Senate districts were not considered. The Louisiana Supreme Court subsequently dismissed a challenge to the new house districts, which went into effect with the December state primary. Although the state constitution requires reapportionment every 10 years, none has been enacted since 1921.

MAINE

On November 5, 1963, the voters adopted a constitutional amendment designed to increase the urban representation in the state house. On January 17, 1964, a special session of the legislature reapportioned the house pursuant to the constitutional amendment. No action has been taken in regard to the senate, the composition of which is based on some nonpopulation factors.

*MARYLAND

The Maryland Court of Appeals has held that both houses do not have to be apportioned according to a population standard. However, the court found that the apportionment of the house constituted invidious discrimination and was invalid. The legislature then apportioned the lower house to reflect population. A case is now pending before the U.S. Supreme Court challenging the court's ruling allowing apportionment of the senate along nonpopulation lines.

MASSACHUSETTS

The state legislature has pending a law which would reapportion the house districts so as to reflect more accurately the existing population. However, the Supreme Judicial Court of Massachusetts has issued an advisory opinion holding this pending legislation unconstitutional. No action has been taken concerning the current senate apportionment which is based on a standard other than strict population.

*MICHIGAN

In 1963, Michigan held a constitutional convention and adopted a new constitution. This new constitution included new apportionment provisions according to which the senate formula considers factors other than population, while the house apportionment is on strictly a population basis. The Michigan Supreme Court had previously held that certain 1952 constitutional amendments were invalid under the Fourteenth Amendment to the U.S. Constitution. However, Justice Stewart of the U.S. Supreme Court had issued an order staying the redistricting order of the Michigan Court. A legislative apportionment committee was appointed to prepare a districting plan. The commission could not agree, and the proposed districting plans were submitted to the Michigan Supreme Court for their decision. The Michigan Supreme Court indicated that it would make no decision pending further guidance from the decisions pending before the U.S. Supreme Court. The Supreme Court acted in June, 1964. On June 22, the Michigan Supreme Court accordingly ordered into effect a reapportionment in which districts for both houses were laid out on the sole basis of population.

Minnesota

In 1958 a federal court held that inequalities in district populations denied citizens equal protection of the laws, but gave the legislature a year in which to act. In its next session the legislature reapportioned for the first time since 1913. Both houses were affected by this legislation.

Mississippi

Recently, a constitutional amendment was approved by the voters reapportioning the state. Both the house and senate were affected by the amendment. However, the amendment still calls for under-representation of the state's four largest urban areas. Prior to the adoption of the constitutional amendment state courts held the existing apportionment law invalid. Litigation is currently pending before the U.S. Supreme Court.

Missouri

Federal court actions have been instituted to force reapportionment of the house, currently weighted heavily towards rural areas. A similar suit has also been filed in the Missouri Supreme Court. No final action has been taken. The senate is apportioned along population lines.

MONTANA

The house was reapportioned in 1961 with each county automatically accorded one member and additional seats distributed according to population. Senate membership is fixed by the constitution at one member per county. No court actions have been instituted.

NEBRASKA

In November, 1962, the voters approved a constitutional amendment changing the constitutional basis for apportionment of the unicameral legislature from a strict population basis to a formula giving 20 to 30 percent weight to geographic area. A federal court has refused to take action on the constitutional amendment until further guide lines have been announced by the U.S. Supreme Court.

NEVADA

A suit has been filed in a federal court seeking the apportionment of the senate on a strict population basis. The senate is presently apportioned to guarantee each county one member. The house was apportioned in 1961 to reflect population. Litigation is also pending in a state court.

NEW HAMPSHIRE

The New Hampshire Supreme Court in July, 1962, held that the apportionment of the senate on the basis of direct taxes paid was valid. Also, the apportionment of the house does not strictly reflect population. Litigation has been filed in federal court asking for legislative reapportionment for the house. This suit is still pending. A constitutional convention has been called for 1964 and the members will be elected March 10, 1964. Recommendations will be made to change the composition of both the house and senate.

NEW JERSEY

The legislature reapportioned its house in 1961 to more accurately reflect population. The senate apportionment scheme allots one seat to each county regardless of population. A suit has been filed in a state court challenging the apportionment of the senate. The action is still pending.

NEW MEXICO

In November, 1963, a unique "weighted voting" scheme was adopted by the legislature. This plan reapportioned the house. Under this plan each of the counties will be guaranteed a seat in the house with the remaining seats distributed according to the method of equal proportions used for the U. S. House. Then each county's representatives are given a share of the total house voting strength (set at 700) which is proportionate to their share of the state's population. This legislative action followed a ruling by a federal court directing that the house apportionment be carried out by December 1, 1963. As of this writing, a state court has eliminated the above weighting requirements but accepted the remainder of the legislation.

*NEW YORK

A federal court in July, 1964, ordered the legislature to enact a reapportionment law by April 1, 1965, and in the meantime to elect a legislature for a one-year term only.

NORTH CAROLINA

A special session of the legislature in October, 1963, adopted legislation reapportioning the senate to reflect more accurately the population. The voters have approved a constitutional amendment which strengthens rural control in the house. A form of a "little federal plan" was recently submitted to the electorate under a constitutional amendment. This amendment was defeated.

NORTH DAKOTA

In 1960 three constitutional amendments were adopted by initiative procedure. Both houses were affected. The house was reapportioned by the 1961 legislature, but this was set aside by the North Dakota Supreme Court. The 1963 constitution again reapportioned the house. Current apportionment under constitutional provision is by area alone in the senate and by area and population in the house. A suit has been instituted in a federal court seeking to set aside the constitutional provisions and also the apportionment made under them by the 1963 legislature. The action is still pending. After the decision by the state supreme court and before the 1963 reapportionment, a federal court has declined to act until the state supreme court had passed on the question.

*OHIO

A federal court upheld the apportionment of the house by area, but providing that each county shall have at least one representative. The senate is apportioned on a population basis.

*OKLAHOMA

A federal court ordered a specific plan of reapportionment, reapportioning both houses or roughly a strict population basis. This action on the part of the court ordering reapportionment by judicial decree came after the legislature failed to abide by the court's prior order. This was the first time that a federal court has actually reapportioned a state legislature by judicial decree employing a plan formulated by the court itself. This case is now pending before the U.S. Supreme Court, and the latter court has stayed the lower federal court's order.

OREGON

A 1961 apportionment act was held invalid by the state supreme court as violative of the population standard of the state constitution. Pursuant to the constitution, the court decreed a reapportionment in October, 1961. A "little federal plan" was rejected by the voters in 1962.

PENNSYLVANIA

In December, 1963, the legislature passed a reapportionment bill reducing population inequalities in both the house and senate. A federal court recently invalidated this legislation in that it discriminates against urban counties in limiting senatorial representation.

Rhode Island

In June, 1963, a special legislative session passed a house reapportionment plan, but the plan was vetoed by the governor. A suit is pending in federal court challenging the constitutionality of the current districts. At present, neither the house nor the senate is apportioned on a strict population basis. The state supreme court had ruled previously that the legislature is bound to reapportion itself on the basis of the 1960 census. In 1961 the legislature apportioned the house according to population.

South Carolina

There has been no litigation or legislation since *Baker*. The house districts, as revised in 1961, have a population range of 3 to 1. The senate is composed of a member from each county and has population disparities of 50 to 1.

South Dakota

The legislature was apportioned in 1961 on a population basis. The South Dakota Supreme Court ruled invalid a petition seeking to put the new apportionment to a referendum in 1962.

Tennessee

Subsequent to *Baker* v. *Carr,* the state legislature apportioned members of the house and senate. However, a federal court held that the act did not comply with the state constitution and suggested that the 1963 legislature pass an act which would comply with the constitution with the help of guide lines prescribed by the court in its opinion. This court said that one house could deviate from a strict population as long as the other house is apportioned by population. The 1963 legislature reapportioned both the house and senate. The apportionment of the house was based partially on the number of qualified voters in each county and district, but the apportionment of senators was not [based upon the number of qualified voters in each district]. In October, 1963, a federal court held that the acts did not meet the requirements of the constitution and were not in accord with the guide lines prescribed by the court. An appeal has been filed in the U.S. Supreme Court.

TEXAS

The legislature reapportioned the house in 1961, but rural areas are still overrepresented in both the house and senate. Litigation is pending in a federal court.

UTAH

Legislation was passed in 1963 affecting the apportionment in both houses. As a general rule apportionment in Utah is based on population as far as the house is concerned, excepting that under the constitution each county is entitled to one representative. Apportionment of the senate is based on area and population. A suit is pending in a federal court challenging the apportionment setup.

VERMONT

The Vermont Supreme Court held, in July, 1962, that the then existing apportionment was unconstitutional and retained jurisdiction to afford the legislature an opportunity to take action. The Vermont constitution provides that senators be apportioned among the several counties according to population. The apportionment of the house is based primarily on area. Subsequent to the state supreme court action the legislature reapportioned the senate. There is presently pending before a federal court a case challenging the constitutionality of both houses of the legislature.

*VIRGINIA

Virginia's 1962 apportionment act was declared unconstitutional by a federal court. The court fixed a deadline for the legislature to reapportion both houses by population as prescribed in the state constitution. This case has been appealed to the U.S. Supreme Court and the decision of the lower federal court has been stayed. In a separate action, a state court dismissed a suit against the state's apportionment, holding that the apportionment was constitutional.

*Washington

In the general election held in November, 1956, the voters approved an initiative reapportioning the state's legislative districts. These districts compose the areas from which both houses of the legislature are selected (generally two representatives and one senator to each district). A federal court had ordered the legislature to reapportion in the 1963 session. When the legislature failed to reapportion, the court declared all present legislative districts void, thus leaving both houses of the legislature to run at large. The decisions were appealed to the U.S. Supreme Court, and subsequently the order requiring the legislature to run at large was temporarily held in abeyance pending final determination by the Supreme Court.

West Virginia

In 1962 the legislature passed a statute ignoring the state constitutional provision which requires that counties under a certain proportion of population be joined with other counties as delegate districts. Thereupon, suits were filed in both federal and state courts, and the State Supreme Court ruled the statute unconstitutional. The legislature then created delegate districts for the smaller, less populous counties in an effort to comply with the constitutional requirement.

Wisconsin

The Wisconsin Supreme Court declared unconstitutional the existing senate and house districts and ordered the Governor and the legislature to reapportion by May 1, 1964. The state constitution requires apportionment according to population. The governor and the legislature could not agree on new legislative districts, and so, in May, the Wisconsin court itself reapportioned the districts—an unprecedented move, the first in the nation.

Wyoming

In 1963 the Legislature passed legislation reapportioning both houses. The senate apportionment is not based strictly on population nothwithstanding a constitutional provision requiring such a standard. This act is in litigation before a federal court, but a decision has not yet been handed down.

☆ Bibliography ☆

BOOKS

Baker, Gordon E., *Rural Versus Urban Political Power,* New York, Random House, 1955.

Baker, Gordon E., *The Politics of Reapportionment in Washington,* New York, Holt, Rinehart and Winston, 1960.

David, Paul T., and Ralph Eisenberg, *Devaluation of the Urban and Suburban Vote,* 2 vols., Charlottesville, Bureau of Public Administration, University of Virginia, 1961–1962.

Grazia, Alfred de, *Essay on Apportionment and Representative Government,* Washington, Institute for Social Science Research, 1963.

Havard, William C., and Loren P. Beth, *The Politics of Mis-Representation,* Baton Rouge, Louisiana State University Press, 1962.

Jewell, Malcolm E. *et al., The Politics of Reapportionment,* New York, Atherton, 1962.

Lamb, Karl *et al., Apportionment and Representative Institutions, the Michigan Experience,* Washington, Institute for Social Science Research, 1963.

Larson, James E., *Reapportionment and the Courts,* Bureau of Public Administration, University of Alabama, 1962.

Steiner, Gilbert, and Samuel Gove, *Legislative Politics in Illinois,* Urbana, University of Illinois Press, 1960.

DOCUMENTS

Advisory Commission on Intergovernmental Relations, *Apportionment of State Legislatures,* Washington, the Commission, 1962.

California Assembly Committee on Elections and Reapportionment, *Report,* Sacramento, the Assembly, 1961.

California Study Commission on Senate Apportionment, *Report,* Sacramento, the Commission, 1962.

Council of State Governments, *Legislative Reapportionment in the States, a Summary of Action Since June, 1960,* Chicago, the Council, 1962.

National Municipal League, *Compendium on Legislative Apportionment,* 2nd ed., New York, the League, 1962.

National Municipal League, *Court Decisions on Legislative Apportionment,* 7 vols., New York, the League, 1962–1964.

PAMPHLETS

Baker, Gordon E., *State Constitutions: Reapportionment,* New York, National Municipal League, 1960.

Boyd, William, *Patterns of Apportionment,* New York, National Municipal League, 1962.

David, Paul T. and Ralph Eisenberg, *State Legislative Redistricting,* Chicago, Public Administration Service, 1962.

McKay, Robert, *Reapportionment and the Federal Analogy,* New York, National Municipal League, 1962.

Twentieth Century Fund, *One Man-One Vote, A Statement of Principals,* New York, the Fund, 1963.

Wells, David, *Legislative Representation in New York State,* New York, International Ladies' Garment Workers' Union, 1963.

ARTICLES

Bickel, Alexander, "Reapportionment and Liberal Myths," *Commentary,* June, 1963, pp. 481–483.

Dixon, Robert G., "Legislative Apportionment and the Federal Constitution," *Law and Contemporary Problems,* Summer, 1962, pp. 329–389.

Goldberg, Arthur L., "The Statistics of Malapportionment," *Yale Law Journal,* Nov., 1962, pp. 90–106.

Hacker, Andrew, "Reapportionment: Who Will Benefit?," *Challenge,* Feb., 1963, pp. 4–7.

Hamilton, Howard D. *et al.,* "Legislative Reapportionment in Indiana: Some Observations and a Suggestion," *Notre Dame Lawyer,* May, 1960, pp. 368–404.

Hanson, Royce, "Courts in the Thicket: the Problem of Judicial Standards," *American University Law Review,* Jan., 1963, pp. 1–31.

Israel, Jerold, "On Charting a Course Through the Mathematical Quagmire," *Michigan Law Review,* Nov., 1962.

Lewis, Anthony, "Legislative Apportionment and the Federal Courts," *Harvard Law Review*, April, 1958, pp. 1057–1098.

Maslow, Will, "Reapportionment: Breaking the Rural Strangle Hold," *Nation,* April 6, 1963, pp. 282–285.

McCloskey, Robert, "The Reapportionment Case," *Harvard Law Review,* Nov., 1962, p. 54.

McKay, Robert, "Political Thickets and Crazy Quilts," *Michigan Law Review,* Feb., 1963, pp. 647–710.

Miller, H. H., "The City Vote and the Rural Monopoly," *Atlantic Monthly,* Oct., 1962, pp. 61–65.

Neal, Phil C., "*Baker* v. *Carr:* Politics in Search of Law," *Supreme Court Review*, 1962, p. 252.

Silva, Ruth C., "Apportionment of the New York Legislature," *American Political Science Review,* Dec., 1961, pp. 870–881.

Titus, J. E., "Democracy and Metropolitan Representation," *Southwestern Social Science Quarterly,* June, 1963, pp. 25–34.

Tyler, Gus, "Court Versus Legislature," *Law and Contemporary Problems,* Summer, 1962, pp. 390–407.

Tyler, Gus, "The Problem of Malapportionment: a Symposium on *Baker* v. *Carr,*" *Yale Law Journal,* Nov., 1962, pp.7–106.

Tyler, Gus, "Reapportionment Series," *Notre Dame Lawyer,* June, 1963, pp. 367–429; Aug., 1963, pp. 487–517.

Current developments are reported in the "Representation" section of the *National Civic Review,* monthly.

☆ Index ☆